R. M. Williams was born ... . started work as a lime burner in Victoria, then moved to Western Australia, where as camel boy for the missionary William Wade, he explored the Gibson Desert and the Musgrave, Mann, Tompkinson and Petermann Ranges. William Wade was the inspirational subject of R. M. Williams' book *A Song in the Desert* published in 1998.

R. M. has worked as well-sinker, stockman, tea planter (in the New Guinea highlands), miner, cattle trader and drover, but he is most widely known for the manufacturing enterprise that bears his name. He lives in the Arcadia Valley in Queensland, where he breeds cattle.

ALSO BY R. M. WILLIAMS

A Song in the Desert

True stories from one of Australia's greatest folk heroes

R. M. Williams

I Once Met a Man

Angus&Robertson
An imprint of HarperCollins*Publishers*

Angus&Robertson

An imprint of HarperCollins*Publishers,* Australia

First published in Australia by Angus & Robertson Publishers in 1989
Imprint edition published in 1992
This A&R Classics edition published in 1995
by HarperCollins*Publishers* Pty Limited
ABN 36 009 913 517
A member of the HarperCollins*Publishers* (Australia) Pty Limited Group
www.harpercollins.com.au

HarperCollins*Publishers*
25 Ryde Road, Pymble, Sydney, NSW 2073, Australia
31 View Road, Glenfield, Auckland 10, New Zealand
77-85 Fulham Palace Road, London W6 8JB, United Kingdom
2 Bloor Street East, 20th floor, Toronto, Ontario, M4W 1A8, Canada
10 East 53rd Street, New York NY 10022, USA

National Library of Australia Cataloguing-in-Publication data:

Williams, R. M. (Reginald Murray), 1908– .
I once met a man.
ISBN 0 207 19024 0.
1. Frontier and pioneer life – Australia.
2. Australia – Social life and customs – 20th century.
I. Title.
994.04

Printed and bound in Australia by Griffin Press on 80gsm Econoprint

16 15 14 13 12   04 05 06 07

CONTENTS

INTRODUCTION

Understand, then, that these chapters are concerned with the spirit of men and women from whom something of worth has shone out to make them worthy of record.

You will note that the book is not of deeds, achievement, great honour; just that indefinable something that has no other name in our language but spirit, though other people in other languages have defined it better. It might be worth recording here that the philosophers of all time have arrived at the conclusion that spirit and truth are all.

No attempt has been made to record the life and history of the people of these stories. Sufficient that when men or women move, they carry with them what they are.

 I ONCE MET A MAN . . .

MEN WHO LAID THE RAILS
BUT WHO THEMSELVES LEFT
NO TRACKS

I have written of good men, for good is as good does, but all are not such and at the lower strata of society (which, looking back, was my level) some men are bad, for bad is as bad does.

The train that opened up the dead heart of Australia was called "The Ghan" for the simple reason that it was most used by Afghans. Most people living at Marree, Farina, Oodnadatta, and Alice Springs were Ghans or their descendants, but the time I write of was before the line had passed Oodnadatta, and the Ghan was crowded with potential navvies or pick-and-shovel men. The rail lines of yesterday were all built by hand and the men who followed this particular profession were for the most part muscle men of the wandering type, and some were scum — brutal, hard drinking, fighting men.

How I came to be a passenger with this particular group of labourers going north on the Ghan is lost in the sixty-five years of then and now, but sufficient that in the long, single-gauge carriage with thirty such men, with my swag on the rack, I was heading north. In my book there were few who did not fall into a classification — they were good or bad. I elected to sit with an old grizzled navvy type: Scotty he claimed was his name and I asked no more questions — his rating was written in his face. I classed him as a good old man and we talked.

On the first night going north, as the train rattled its way along, the carriage became rowdy with men getting slowly drunker. Some were swaggering noisily and some were glowering, darkly quarrelsome. One big swarthy animal-type pushed his way to and fro along the aisle, kicking any foot that projected in his way. He marched up and down flourishing a bottle and looking for trouble; every man avoided him. Because I was the youngest and sober, Darky picked on me for nothing at all, and Scotty told him in his Scottish drawl to move on. The man was tall and looked to be very strong — he was the bully type — but Scotty rose and urged him away. Darky punched Scotty in the throat and Scotty fell like a log, never moved then or after — he was dead. It was two hot days to Oodnadatta and by the time we arrived Scotty was too long dead: nobody seemed to want to know about it. The carriage emptied quickly and left me with the dead man; he had, it seemed, died for me. I dug a shallow grave and buried him; months later old Jim Mitchell made a cross of plaster cast and wrote on it "Scotty–1928".

Two days after the train trip, Darky came into the inland mission recreation room where I was playing chess with a man unknown. Others were there, watching. I could see that Darky remembered that I had seen him kill Scotty and I reckoned that, being a witness, I could be next. Darky worked around behind me and my instinct told me that something had to be done quickly. I made an excuse and moved out.

I ONCE MET A MAN . . .

Once outside the hut I ran to my camp and loaded the old Winchester .32. My camp was a bit out of town where old Jim Mitchell had a humpy and Jim offered to be witness if Darky came with intentions. Apparently two guns were enough, for Darky left me alone, but my resolve was strengthened — I had to learn all the dirty tricks that his kind played.

  I ONCE MET A MAN . . .

THE LAST
OF HIS KIND

W hen the rail started north to Alice Springs — the second start after its short burst to Marree in the 1890s — the land west had not been opened up for settlement or if it had no one seemed to take notice. The few who squatted and settled had various unsatisfactory results until 1926, and the boldest took titles but none further than one hundred and fifty miles from the telegraph line.

Anna Creek, with its fourteen thousand square miles, with boundaries only on paper in the lands office, was neighboured by men like old Ly Underdown and Giles, bordered by Lennons and the O'Donoughs, who held land north to the Alberga, but none of these knew, or wanted to know, what lay further west. Even Frank Smith at Tieyon, a bold settler, could not answer questions about the big hills further out, and gave me a quizzing look with the comment, "You want to see all the nudies?" That comment did not rate an answer because I was going to look over the territory west of Tieyon, even if the tribes were in clothes or not. Fact is they were not: pity they ever were. A few blackbirders ventured out into the ranges, a few prospectors, odd explorers: some of these we met on our travels but a horse or camel track was rare, and only one buggy track ever I saw. It did not penetrate far because I backtracked it in curiosity — went as far as Mitchell's Knob, turned back there to station country. Station people told me later it was Basedow.

Little was known about the blacks, but every white man leaving the line had to have horses or camels and a visit somewhere before heading into the west. Fellows like Lasseter made a big notice before they went out gold hunting, everybody (and that did not mean many) knew what was going on. At the time wild dogs were money, which meant that a few loners were poking about within the scope of their ration supplies, but not many of them. For the first two hundred miles we expected to meet up with bagmen but we did not. From the lack of tracks, and there would have to be tracks going into the only big waters on the way, we supposed that we were

I ONCE MET A MAN . . .

alone in that million square miles of country that takes in the Gibson and the Great Victoria Deserts down to the vast stretch of mallee desert belting on the Nullarbor. A lot of empty country, except for the tribes still living as they always had.

The great flat east of the Ernabella Range to the Glen Ferdinand Valley was alive with daisies and geraniums three foot high, the like of which I have not seen since, and there grazing peacefully a couple of thousand sheep — herded or shepherded by unclad nomads and one grizzled old white man. He had a military greatcoat that had seen better days, a seven pound fruit can for a billy, a knife, and nothing more — no swag, no horses, no possessions. Looked cheerful — was amiable, spoke reasonable. Offered that he had come back ways from New South Wales, was going nowhere, needed nothing, lived off mutton, grass bulbs, odd wild fruit. If ever a fellow needed a lesson in survival that was it — I have remembered.

I ONCE MET A MAN . . .

THE HAND THAT CARVED
THE BRAND

Some say that after the seeking the finding pales and there is less pleasure. This is not always so.

After months of looking in likely and unlikely places for a home-site, weary months by packsaddle, lonely roads (for I was not sure what I wanted except to just wander and look), I came upon an old abandoned station, far off the roads.

This was 1953, and the pioneer gravestone told me that the stone was erected in 1942. The bush was taking over the grave and the trees were growing where fields had been. When I saw the old slab huts, the lonely grave under the giant wilgas by the long waterhole, the feeling came that I was home, for there in the old scrap heap were worn out tools, a lifetime of work by a man who had built this place. The man's spirit was brooding over the spot he had loved.

For months I had roamed the outback of Queensland looking for such a place — a place to start again. That the fences were rusted and broken, and the land was overgrown, did not deter me because the man in the grave was long since dead and did not need a critic. He had laboured long and with great courage through the years when Cobb & Co. ran mails, and before that, too, when the only rail service bringing goods was one hundred and twelve miles away by wagon.

For some reason the old man had hidden a bottle in a cave, with invoices of goods that dated back into the last century. I read them and religiously screwed back the bottle cap, but within twelve months the contents were dust. On the roof of a cave, together with Aboriginal paintings, he had left his initials. The date — 1874.

His posts were deep in the rocky ground, each hole a memorial to a thorough painstaking man. It took me twenty years with machinery and help to follow the fifty miles of boundaries that he had cleared and dug by hand. There were no nails, no precious iron in the gates still standing; all mortice and wooden pegs, all wooden hinges and split rails. Story goes that he hacked his own grave from flinty rock, so great was his determination to stay forever in the place he loved, and the coffin he prepared was of hand-cut boards. I am sure he witnessed my years in that place, for I believe in spirits.

When the old man was buried, the eldest son of the eldest son was given the chance to take over the cattle and the station that his grandfather had pioneered. He was alone in the slab-built house with its rough-hewn rooms that had been added as the family grew. The house was very old: the wind whistled at night through the slab walls. Word was (and we have proof) that cattle would not camp at night on the hill across the river. Eerie for a young man alone — he quit. For years the ghost of Hamilton waited for someone to take up his worn-out tools.

Some people buy land to get rich but I had come to stay. In it I saw a place for generations of men who can let the

I ONCE MET A MAN . . .

good earth fall through their fingers and smell the sweetness of rich soil, and love it for the trees it grows and the challenge of its regeneration of forest as soon as the latest settler is tired. We shall not be daunted by the floods that sweep away our fences — rather we shall smell the brown water of the swelling river and know that the grass will grow, and we will be rich in the rewards of labour and the peace of living with nature; this is the heritage I will leave my people.

Some people's lives centre around things and places that mean nothing to others. In the tangle of a brigalow forest, there alone among the lesser trees, grew a giant bottle tree. I measured forty-two feet around the base. Probably centuries old, it hadn't changed, old Ernie said, since granddad found it.

There — see high up is a hole clustered with bees! They have been there for over a hundred years that we know. There is a pride of belonging in the old man's eyes — his tree. Tall, stooped, thin hipped, the kind of man a life in the saddle breeds.

Every time we rode together Ern had something to show me. A tiny hidden rock-hole with enough water to stop and boil the lunchtime quart. It was covered with a rock — his people, long dead, had drunk there before him and kept it covered, it was their place. Deep down in the rugged gorges — lonely, unvisited, where cattle sometimes wandered in good times and outlaw bullocks hid knowing that no man or horse could follow them up the secret paths between the great boulders and steep cliffs — there was a cave. Smoke from centuries of Aboriginal fires had blackened the roof where paintings of spear, boomerang, and generations of dead hands had recorded their possessions. Among the smoky paintings a brand stood out, carved deeply — 4H 1874. Ern looked down, from pointing — see, grandfather was here!

The place was wild, untamed. The hand that carved the brand had bred a son who in turn had ridden those dark scrubs, loved the wilderness, fought drought, flood, and had gone with others to leave his marks among the rocks, the caves, but little else, for forests cut down grow again, cottages crumble. Only his grave remained. Ern stood with me before the grave, the very lonely grave. "My father!" he said.

I was a stranger to that long-loved land, but Ern had a feeling that these places where his father had spent all his years were not to remain unloved, for Kin meets Kind and Knows. He knew the place, his boyhood place, every brigalow scrub and gully, places where cattle hide, for generations of cows had bred there since the last time his father had branded. It did not have to be spoken that just once more he — son of the son of the pioneer — would like to ride again: to throw and tie the wild ones, race through the unraceable places, show the stranger how the old ones rode. That is how it was: when the scrubbers ran, he threw and tied. "These things they loved."

HAROLD

When the Archibald prize was the acme for portrait painters, one of the successful winners was a man of realism; his work hangs in Kings Hall, Canberra, the best of the portraits of Australian Prime Ministers. I doubt that Ivor Hele would bother to exhibit now, since most of the entries have become inexplicable caricatures.

Hele had a brother, Harold, a man I was proud to know as my best friend. Long since mourned, Harold Hele managed Balcanoona Station in the Flinders Ranges, now a wildlife park, part of the Gammon Ranges National Park. His nearest town was Copley, near Leigh Creek. Along the one-hundred-mile dusty road from Balcanoona to Copley, there are a few stations: one is Angepena where Harold's girlfriend lived.

For want of a better choice, I selected a site on this Balcanoona road to dig a well. The search for water for the reserve at Nepabunna was in my hands and this was my first exploration well. Harold travelled this road often and seeing fresh dirt he stopped, walked across to the well site and called down the hole. It was seventy feet deep: looking up, the sky

was a pinpoint. I answered and started up the ladder. There was a windlass on the head but this day I had nobody to pull up the buckets of dirt so that climbing the ladder was part of the exercise, for each load needed a climb up to wind out the bucket. I was very fit, also very dirty. He introduced himself and got to talking about wells and water, and made talk about how better it would be to have help to wind the windlass and pull out the dirt instead of climbing the ladder to pull the bucket to the top to empty it each time. I explained that my wife was pregnant, that help cost money, and that muscle was all I had. Harold offered to help and he did. That hole turned out to be a dry hole and we gave it up.

My camp, closer to Balcanoona, became a gathering place for stockmen from the area — Mt Fitton, Pralna, Wooltana and the Moolawatana sandhills. The camp consisted of a log hut and a bough shed, and all the serious living such as cooking and eating was done at the campfire between the hut and the bough shed. We slept there too. The camp fire area became a sort of battleground where we and all the locals, black and white, tried out our various skills — long jump with weights; catch-as-catch-can fighting; arm wrestles; stick pulls; and all the fun and games that happen when young bucks meet about a fire.

Harold was the main traveller to and fro, to see his girl, and never failed to call and stop a while. For us it was the time when young men dream up their futures, and we imagined a lot about what we could do to improve our coming days. It was a talking point at the camp fire, with this bushman of the long hard days and short pay, that his brother Ivor was living soft in Paris, daubing with paint. I am sorry now that Harold never lived to see his idle brother become the great artist painter that he is. Deep empathy and lasting

friendships are made around the camp fire, and in lonely places we shared many small pleasures and greater confidences. His girl and my girl became friends and the four of us would go to isolated water holes and frolic in the hot evenings, *al fresco*.

Time came when the wells were sunk and events brought separation, but we kept one interest in common, a small gold mine showing promise. Excitement was tense, and when the digging showed evidence of a reef with rich-bearing gold quartz I remember the pleasure we shared. Other shared pleasures, simple things such as the sharpening of a crowbar and getting the temper right: finding native rock to use as sharpening stone; setting a cross-cut saw with the correct angles; the girls chattering about making the best bread and spinning a bit of wool, for Phyllis's father was a wool man and we had plenty of raw material. They used the old fashioned way of spinning on the knee. Doing things and making things, that was more than enough to keep us busy.

A visitor rolled in one night about evening, driving a mule pair, big bay mules, the best I had ever seen. And talk about a saddle for a throne! The man had colour and he had style, one foot on the brake, knee bent, reins across his arm as though he knew that he was boss whatever the mules did. The old four-wheel buggy was like a model-T with a quarter of a million miles on the clock, but there was nothing wrong with the outfit that wire could not hold together, and those mules did not need paint to give shine to their hides — they worked for a man who knew what mules thought about eating. One word and those mules stepped right up to the fire; the owner, using his height, looked down on us and asked about his welcome. We settled that unnecessary question, and he pulled the mules out of harness and came over to the fire where the pot was boiling. No one asked where he came from, no one about us ever did, but Mick stayed the full term of years until that camp broke up. Mick liked making things, and together we drew up lots of patterns of things a bushman used. Harold helped.

I shall always keep Harold Hele alive in my memory: his tall good looks and humble ways, never a word about me being a bagman or Mick being a possible horse thief, like people hinted. He looked up to ability as a man should, carried sticks for the fire without asking, and when he brought the meat, it always seemed like we were doing him a favour for letting him give it to us.

One night we sang and laughed the evening away and believed in tomorrow, but for Harold it never came. He went down the shallow mine to put in an early shot and without warning a hanging rock crushed him as it fell, and the light for all of us went out for many a day, but we still remember.

RED

It was a time of great stress to the western world — 1929. Other nations had lately been through upheavals that had brought havoc to their land and poverty to their people. A sixth of the world's land mass was under a new regime that my old mother would say could not succeed because they were godless; I was not so sure. It was a strategic time for change in the capitals of pelf and power; a time to bring the rising tide of workers' unrest to a halt, and halt it did. One day we were working, the next undone; out of work and asking with many others for our names to be put down on the unemployed register for a job. Young men do not yet understand the machinations of power, any more than the ant underfoot knows what inspired the motion of the man who trod on it.

There were thousands of us lighting fires on the riverbanks, sheltering in public places, riding the trains illegally, begging, thieving, and barely surviving. We were blind, confused, desperate, but destitution does not know defeat. In such condition lies the mainspring of man the survivor, and like our ancient forefathers emerging from the caves we collected our long neglected weapons of hereditary initiative and surged out to see what could be done.

"Ah!" you say. "What were your women doing while you were away looking?" There was no dole in 1929 only 10, 2 and ¼ — ten pounds of flour, two of sugar and a quarter pound of tea, with a meat ration once a fortnight. Those evicted from their new homes lived with thousands of others in tents on the riverbanks, and those of us who cared sent survival money back home when we could. We were learning, but this story is not about women, nor about our devious ways of making a penny, it's about a man I called Red. He did not give me, his travelling mate, a name and I never asked.

We met at a place called Clare, the place, incidentally, where my great-grandfather settled when he landed in Australia off the ship from Wales. We were camped one night in the shelter of an overhanging roof on the dark side, for the law had a habit of hounding us on. It was drizzling rain and firewood was not plentiful but I had a fire, as was and is my habit — nothing seems too lonely if a camp fire is going.

Red popped his head around the corner and asked the usual! "Come in?" A question, an announcement, a challenge, if you can get the vernacular of the men of the road.

"Right!" Again the acceptance, for not everyone was welcome at my fire. I had already been bashed once but Red sounded regular. He dumped his miserable thin swag which was even smaller than mine and I prided myself as travelling light. I had stale bread, bummed from the bakery and Red had a few brown bananas and a shirt full of apples, lately hanging on the trees close by. It wasn't much, but the trade union of the road had strict rules about sharing food. The haves of that era did not subscribe to the sharing, although to give the butchers and the bakers credit, they were always good for something, even if the bread or the sausages were past caring for.

I ONCE MET A MAN . . .

Daylight and Red initiated me into his routine. His workshop consisted of a small round sharpening stone, and with this equipment Red gave housewives an assurance of the most professional kind that he could sharpen their kitchen knives for a penny, or their scissors for threepence, or, if they had roses that needed pruning, one penny per rose bush. Careful not to let them see how elementary were his tools, Red would take the knives or the scissors around the corner or into the shade. Give him credit, he could make the dullest knife better than just sharp and with great skill he could make scissors cut silk, a sample of which he always collected from his more affluent customers. His own pocket-knife was always razor sharp and he could persuade the untutored housewife that a good water-shedding angular cut was better and more professional than a horizontal cut on a rose stem, hence the advisability of using a knife. He of course did not have secateurs.

By the end of the second day we — that is he, Red — had worked Clare over and it was time to leave. We had unfortunately visited the sergeant's wife, begging support for our trade, and the sergeant, being a lenient man but still doing his duty as a policeman, advised us (tramps!) to move on. We headed for Burra, an old mining town and not a prosperous town. Here we found the temper of the not long-suffering citizens overexposed to the travelling swagman. Probably they had reason to fear the thieving gypsies of the depression: we did no good, but necessity must.

Red used his expertise on the local fruit shop. His spiel went like this: "I wonder, sir," (with emphasis on the sir) "have you got any speckled spoiled or spoiled fruit!" The answer was a bit drastic for the owner rang the local constable who arrived before we had understood the danger, and Red and I were promptly locked up on the grounds of "insufficient means of support" and charged with vagrancy. We ate well that night and for three days and nights we had no problems of food and shelter. On the third day we were released with advice to leave town.

Red suggested that we head east for, said he, the Murray River is not far and the people on the river have been battlers and know about necessity. So we headed east. Those who have studied a map will know, as I learned, that there is a barren stretch between Burra and the Murray River. Although few, if any, walk that stretch these days, the 1920s were still horse-and-buggy days and we had no horse. Those who had model-T cars, or better, were not picking up potentially dangerous tramps, so we walked!

The first night was not too bad as we had eaten and slept well as guests of His Majesty but, with another long day's walk ahead of us and no tuckerbag, we were ready to beg at the first homestead. It was prosperous looking but I suppose, like us, the station people were on hard times and not disposed to give handouts. The answer we got was a pack of dogs that looked as hungry as we were, and we did not stay.

The dogs did not come past the garden fence and, as luck would have it, the rambling station and woolshed and machinery sheds were scattered over a wide area, among which scratched some ducks, hens and turkeys. Red had vast experience and gave me the benefit of his superior skills, as a man of the road. Turkeys are slow creatures and Red was quick: with a swift lunge he took an unsuspecting turkey by its long neck, thus effectively stifling its noise, and with the other hand grasped its two legs. Thus burdened, he asked me to close ranks and we marched humbly and silently along the road toward the Murray River. Red used the mud of a roadside dam and plastered the now dispatched turkey thickly with dirt.

His camp fire was huge and when it had burned low he buried the turkey deep in the coals and left it to cook for two hours after sundown. I do not know if the caller at our camp that night was a station spy but if he was he did not see a feather or a sign of a turkey cooking. Red was both an experienced thief and an experienced cook.

As the rooftops of the town of Morgan came into sight, Red became uneasy and his conversation went something like this: "I think we had better give Morgan a miss, I have been there before!" That was all, but I understood.

We trudged on through Barmera and Berri to Renmark making better-than-average knife and scissor money on the way and looking forward to large spoils in the big town. Red managed to snaffle a sharpening stone for me and both of us prospered. We were camping between the boilers on the edge of the river at the pumping plant. We were out of sight, and right alongside was a fine orange garden. Since those days, all oranges have had to be measured by the criteria of Renmark navels. I wonder is it just the taste?

The time came for us to move and Red was not liking the long hike, for his home was many miles away. One night Red confided that he was going to travel in style and, to demonstrate his vehicle, lifted a willow branch hanging over the river and produced a new bicycle from the muddy depths of the river. He left me there despising my honourable but humble steps as he pedalled by and I walked. Red's home was Marble Bar in Western Australia, so I could not begrudge him the need of wheels.

BILL GREGORY

Bill Gregory lived alone (well, almost). He confided that he had six children away south at school. Tall, sunburned, drooping moustache, wearing lines of his long years as a camel driver on his face: rugged, craggy, a man alone.

Camels were going out and the merchant he worked for, Wallis Fogarty, gave him the option "Drive a truck or . . .". Bill fought those old Reos and Dodges over the no road to Alice Springs and beyond. Broken axles, differentials, gear boxes — every part of the new transport was likely to (and often did) pack it in. With a camel driver's patience, Bill would light his camp fire and wait perhaps a week, often a month, for help. He carried a lot of water — it was the way his kind survived.

When Bill was away and I was in town, his house, only one room and verandah, was mine. Old Fox, a worn-out, chewed-up camel driver, lived on the verandah. Bill kept him going for old times' sake and the memory of the day he had pulled Bill out from under a bull camel that was trying to kill him. For his part, Fox was chewed up badly by the great fangs of the angry bull. Bill would not forget. Mostly drunk, Fox was a man who had been there and done it all. I learned a lot from Fox.

In the one room there was a long table and on the end of the table a pressure kerosene lamp. At night men gathered around the table to play cooncan; the winner of every hand paid the lamp box and Bill educated his family on the contents, so he said. I saw his black book once; the record of the lamp money was impressive.

One of his chores when he was home was a duty to the girls who ran the butcher's shop. The Underdown girls, fresh from school but bush-bred and ambitious, served the town with meat, some of it killed kosher with a Mohammedan prayer. This meat, I know, got mixed up with the sheep and goats Bill killed. When Bill was away, I took a turn to cut the goats' throats and hang the meat on the hooks for the girls — never with a prayer. Every night at eleven o'clock cooncan stopped and the few stayed to play poker. Bill never played after eleven.

The police station was very close but Virgo, the lone sergeant, never interfered with the illegal saloon. He had to live with these men and the players were no respecters of the law; rough, wild characters most of them, but they knew a top man and Virgo was a man to listen to if he spoke, which was seldom.

Sixty-five years later there are Gregorys about. I wonder if they have heard tell of their great-grandfather.

MICK O'DONOHUE

On the far boundary of the station country west of Oodnadatta, pioneers selected huge areas of part desert country as grazing land for their cattle. Perhaps it was in hopes of being cattle owners for without exception they were poor men. Their early years were financed by shepherding a few sheep and selling dingo scalps to the government.

When I passed through the area in the early 1920s, I found that the most elaborate station homestead was at Granite Downs where Mick O'Donohue had put together a mud and stone room, with a fireplace for an old wood-burning stove. The lavatory arrangements consisted of four short poles with three bullock hides nailed on three sides and no door. Mount Chandler and Wantabella Swamp were tin sheds, and Moorilyana a bit better with a dirt floor and a shed divided into two rooms. The water at Moorilyana was good; the soakage well was only ten feet deep and the granite white water was sweet. I went back there twenty years later to get a drink of the sweet white water but the soak was fallen in and the house shed was gone, as were all the other original settlers' humpies.

Until the law forbade it, all this area was held by men who had black girls and half-caste children. The half-caste children are middle-aged or older now, but through the good work of two pioneer mission women, Hyde and Harris, the children turned out to be good citizens. The law of that time required whites to legally marry the gins or send them back to the tribe — it was a cruel law as the history of the people of this time and area, now being written, will show.

Passing through Granite Downs with a string of camels — going west into an area that was little known except for the diaries of Giles and Warburton — I pulled up and camped with Mick O'Donohue. Mick lived about as rough as can be but he was a philosopher. All his life Mick lived on the far edge of civilisation, never quite part of it. He cooked with wood, went barefoot, and the diet was meat — roasted, boiled, corned, fried, minced, but for the most part corned and boiled. I do believe he liked the company of blacks better than whites, certainly the female blacks because not too many of the young Aboriginals were welcome about the place.

Not being one to order from the storekeeper (Wallis Fogarty at Oodnadatta), Mick did not buy wire; he had no fences, therefore had no fences to mend. Most bushmen used wire for mending everything, hence the words "Cobb and Co", an expression meaning a wire twitch. Mick used greenhide from the beasts he killed. Most of his gear was greenhide, partly tanned by himself — all his ropes were greenhide, pack bags and packsaddles were greenhide, he harnessed camels and his harness was greenhide.

Not having wire or bolts, Mick made his stockyard from lengths of mulga stood on end in a trench — the result was quite effective. For gates, he used wooden hinges and pegs of wood to hold split rails. These gates were masterpieces

I ONCE MET A MAN . . .

of ingenuity. The cattle troughs were cut from logs of gum and very durable — there are still some around after a century of use.

Mick had a way of making steel for knives, which could interest a modern steelmaker or blacksmith. He would make a hot wood fire and starting with any pig iron, heat the iron white hot in the coals, then beat it flat and double it and keep on doing this until the iron was impregnated with carbon. The final result was carbon impregnated iron, which of course is steel. His steel knives were good, very good; the handles he carved himself from a wood that looked like a droopy mulga.

His way of making dough did not require an expensive dish for he mixed the flour on a bag which got crusty but seemed to last indefinitely. Salt and flour seemed to be the only concessions he made to expense; sugar was a luxury that he seldom indulged, but he must have invested in rolls of calico at some time because the gins about the place had calico, loose fitting muu-muu type of one-piece dresses. I don't think Mick required modesty from his dark girls but passers-by might! Still there were few passers-by in those days and those that continued west certainly did not see anything to cover the female form. It is doubtful if any great virtue accrues from hiding behind calico. The tribal people behaved in a very modest manner requiring no hiding place for how God had made them.

Mick offered me half his kingdom to stay but I still had a "world to conquer". So I dug his well, listened to his philosophy, rode his boundaries and went on. A few things he said linger: "Men fight for money, then for power." And, "What is the Kingdom of God that is within you?" Mick wondered.

I ONCE MET A MAN . . .

CHARLIE

The mustering team comprised eight men, all half-caste Aboriginals except Charlie. He was tall with curly hair, no doubt of mixed blood but proud to be an Aboriginal. His people probably came from the ocean islands, perhaps descended from those who mixed with the early inhabitants of Australia.

The muster was what is known as a bangtail muster, named from the practice of cutting the end of a cow's tail to distinguish it from others coming through the yards. Having already been counted, the bangtailed beast is not confused with the newly mustered cattle.

The country being mustered was rough and heavily timbered, dense with wattle bushes, making it difficult to gather wild cattle. And they *were* wild, hadn't been yarded for years — several generations in some cases.

The boys loved this dashing through the scrub, throwing bulls by the tail, tying the wild one by the legs, knocking off their horns, piercing the nose for pegs or putting greenhide blinds over their eyes and leading them home.

So agile was Charlie and so confident of his own survival ability that when on one occasion, where I chanced to be witness, a young cow we were chasing stopped in a clearing and turned ready with her sharp horns to fight, Charlie, with no near trees to climb, ground-tied his horse and let the cow charge him. At the last moment, before impact, he leaped clear over and away. He never did tie that cow but was smart enough to know that cows fight with their eyes open and that her horns were needle sharp.

After the muster I needed someone to help clean up these wild cattle, and Charlie was my choice. He was a good partner and his natural abilities were far above any that have since come to my notice. Riding through the bush he read the signs of nature, understood the tracks, observed what most would never see. After many months during which we never tired of chasing the outlaw cattle, the numbers of wild ones dwindled and Charlie got restless to try himself out as a fighting man. We built a full size rope ring of professional size, installed punching bags, bought gloves and set about readying Chas for his career as a glove man. He fought all he could meet and soon needed a wider field, which meant entering the boxing world in a professional manner.

It seemed that he would not be stopped in his climb to the top of his weight class until — almost there — he was outpointed by a young Sydney fighter. Charlie never fought again but his face remained unmarked and he was ready now for other things.

Without teaching or help of any kind, Charlie began to paint — portraits, animals and birds. He was very good but the art business is a fashion world where few eat well and most starve. Charlie got a paid job, married and because of his fighting record became a supervisor of Aboriginal hostels.

When I see an eagle caged, I think of Charlie. All those years — nine to five, pacing his restricted office, his mind roaming the wild bushland. It will not be for long now, for the cage will soon be unlocked and I believe that he will not be the second Namatjira but the first Charlie Chambers. This is his version of his future.

Charlie lives now in a lonely, wild place where I keep him in canvas. He can watch the eagles soar without envy, listen to the wild dogs howl and know that, like them, he is free, watching nature "paint on a ten league canvas".

VIRGO

Sergeant of police at Oodnadatta in the 1920s, a one man station. If he had a first name I never heard it. Tall, dour and very thin. My first meeting was at Moorilyana, two hundred miles west of the end of the rail line — Oodnadatta — then capital city of the far north, or so it seemed to me. He was shepherding a long string of naked Aboriginals, all chained and hurrying to keep up with the camel he, Virgo, rode.

The memory lingers.

Far to the north there was an Aboriginal extermination programme going on. An old prospector called Brooks had been murdered and put down a rabbit burrow west of Alice Springs, and whole families of blacks had been shot in reprisal. Whites in the west carried hand guns in those days and used them. It was my first trip into the not-yet-settled west and I was going out past the last frontier cattle station when Virgo passed me, going east back to Oodnadatta. The wild tribes were hostile and understandably so as they could still remember Giles and Warburton going through fifty years before.

That was 1926 and now, just sixty-odd years later, a

I ONCE MET A MAN . . .

document has come into my hand about a child Virgo took from her mother. It was the law that half-caste girls had to be taken into state custody and Ruth, for that was her given name, recalls that Virgo caught up with her mother camped on the Hamilton River and took her into police custody. I knew Ruth later — her real name was Molly Lennon and her benefactors gave her to my wife as a servant. We kept her until she married a boy called Coulthard; Ruth had thirteen children and is still alive. Her story is an interesting reflection of the Virgo era. (Her book is just now being written.)

Virgo must have sensed my feelings about the way he was obliged to handle blacks because when the law of that year allowed he sent a new assistant, who had lately arrived to help keep peace with striking rail construction gangs, to collect my weapons. There was no telephone, no radio, no regular mail but the message given me by the Aboriginals told loud and clear that he was on his way west by fast camel to collect my weapons and/or me. Virgo believed that he had the finest, fastest, best equipped camel patrol in Australia — saddles were fine pieces of craftsmanship, his water canteens were made from heavy leather that rode snug and quietly. The five bullock camels were all tall fast movers.

I, in turn, believed that my team was equal and as it resolved he did not catch up with me. Try as he might, he never got nearer than a hundred miles. To avoid further trouble I gave

myself up a year later. Virgo turned in his chair as I entered his office and all he said was "You".

Virgo was never a nuisance to gamblers and kept the peace. His handling of the big strike when five hundred navvies got rough was a classic — he allowed the crowd to illegally board the train going south, stopped the train twenty miles out and threw the navvies off and let them walk back. I was in the water tank above the carriages — he missed me.

Youth, as always, will disagree with the law, but looking back I would say that Virgo was not only a fine man but withal a great pioneer policeman.

PADDY
THE TRACK RIDER

Five miles north of Oodnadatta there stands a crooked pole placed there by the overland telegraph line builders last century. Close by, only a rifle shot away, is the "Angle Pole" water hole, on the Neales River (or creek), with a few straggly trees along its banks. The land is held by Todmorden Station, a large cattle station and home last century of the famous Breadon horse breeding establishment, a spread then of ten thousand square miles, still more than half that, or it was when Paddy De Conlay rode boundaries on its southern end and camped at Angle Pole. His camp consisted of a line of packsaddles and a few bushes to keep the wind off his fire.

My introduction to Paddy was dramatic. His camp was on the west side of the waterhole and mine was across the water to the east. He was away tracking stray cattle when I pulled in to camp and that afternoon, as he pulled his packs off and built a fire, I noticed a single rider come in from the east on my side of the creek. I reckoned it would be a Todmorden or Macumba rider. The newcomer slipped off his horse about two hundred yards from me and in his hand he had a rifle. I was slow in picking up his intentions but quick enough to move when he started firing at Paddy across the waterhole. His first shot missed but it stirred Paddy into action and within seconds Paddy was down behind the packs and had started shooting — both had old single shot Winchesters, not great weapons at that distance. My armament was an old single-barrel shotgun and a small automatic — good for twenty-five yards at best, but it was handy. When the stranger found that he was likely to be fighting on two fronts he mounted and galloped away.

Next day a group of us including Paddy were in Ly Underdown's butcher shop. Ly was behind the counter and we were squatting on the floor, just a gathering of locals discussing various topics. A stranger — apparently *the* stranger — pushed open the door and Paddy jumped to his feet. The newcomer had a knife in his boot pouch and he jumped Paddy — quickest thing I ever saw was Paddy's response: he kicked the fellow in the stomach and hit him as he doubled. The knife fell and Paddy was on it like a cat and by this time we were all on our feet. Ly came over the counter with his meat cleaver, the only weapon he had handy. The door was open and our intruder just vanished — his horse was ground-tied ten feet away and again, for the second time in two days, he had missed out on whatever feud he had with De Conlay. "Over a gin," was all I ever got out of Paddy.

A few years later Paddy asked me to be a witness for him at the registry office in Adelaide. I asked him where he had met the girl: "Picked her up," another three word discussion. That was Paddy — he never wasted words but, my, he could sing if the occasion was right.

About the time of the incident in Ly Underdown's shop, the then Governor-General, Lord Stonehaven, was visiting Oodnadatta to open the new train line to Alice Springs. We were killing a beast on the Angle Pole waterhole for meat to be delivered to Lord Stonehaven's train and the boys had brought down some grog; everybody was merry, we enjoyed the rare occasion. When the train steamed down the new-laid rails past our camp, we awoke to the fact that the meat was still hanging from a tree, we had no meat bags to put it in and only our horses to deliver it by. The problem was solved when somebody thought of the fresh hide from the newly killed beast — we wrapped the best of the meat in the still wet hide and, with blood dripping, I delivered the parcel to the train. My well remembered speech to the one who came to the train steps — the Lord himself — was, "Here's your meat, mister." No doubt he told the tale in the House of Lords; give him his due he took the parcel with goodwill and dignity. That was sixty-four years ago and I still remember the scene and the old chap taking the blood-dripping parcel.

And Paddy was still singing his Irish collection when I got back to camp.

OGILVIE
THE POET

In all my shiftings from place to place, and they have been many, I am surprised to discover that there is still with me the Ogilvie file: letters from him and his wife; poems written in his own neat hand, still unpublished; letters from his agent J.A. Allen of No. 1 Buckingham Palace Road, London. Great Australian poet, Ogilvie; there is music in his verse, "Kings of the Earth when we Ride", "Saddle for a Throne".

Early years, when I was publishing bush verse and anything in the way of stories from the romantics of lonely places, came verses with "Author Unknown". This intrigued me and, in due course, I uncovered the source of this remembered but "Author Unknown" verse. A lot of it proved to come from a series of books published last century by a wandering outback poet, written as it were on horseback. The book was called *Fair Girls and Grey Horses*, and another, *Over the Grass*, and yet another and another until, it seemed, this forgotten man must be a hidden Kipling. And so it proved to be.

I had a son at school at MIT in Boston, America, and yearly tried to visit him. On the way I decided to see if Ogilvie was still alive, reputed to live in the highlands of Scotland, at Selkirk. Took a cab in London and gave the instructions, "Selkirk please". The London cabbie looked hard at me and looked up his referdex. With a defeated look he explained that, as a Londoner of fifty years' experience, he was sure that no such place existed. I explained that Scotland could not be far, for I had heard that, end to end, England was only five hundred miles, and that was only Oodnadatta to Adelaide. Did he want to go to Selkirk? Yes he did, but (and with many buts) he explained that there would be snow in Scotland, and it was way out of his territory. We hummed and hawed about it all, and with the spirit of adventure still not quite dead, decided to borrow chains for his wheels. Away we went to see Ogilvie in Scotland. Past Manchester, past the lakes, on to Glasgow, and through the towering streets of Edinburgh; on, on, up into the snow drifts we ploughed, chains on the wheels now, and at last to the streets of Selkirk.

Ogilvie had inherited his father's title of laird, and with it a cottage on the estate. There he was, still the same pipe smoking old man, remembering the dusty hot plains of Nelangie and his mates of long ago — "The Breaker", "Dukabrook", "Glen Idle". What a breath of Australia I brought; together we decided which verse would go into a new book and what it would be called. The title decided and the odd verses discarded, *Saddle for a Throne* it was. Since that day, tens of thousands of copies of Ogilvie's verse have been placed again in their rightful place of high esteem by the people of Australia. Ogilvie is dead but his verse will live forever in the hearts of those who love the brown lands.

JEANIE
FORBES

Lonton was a crowded slum even in 1902, and the area around the Bow Cathedral the dingiest slum of all. To say that you were born within the sound of the Bow bells proclaimed that you were a true Londoner. Jean was born there, eldest of a poor but decent family — too many mouths to feed, so that for Jean there were no extras. In 1920, Jean emigrated to Australia on a crowded ship little better than the convict hulks of the previous century, a slow journey, making landfall in Sydney a welcome relief.

Work was found at once — pretty girls were in great demand for the station places in the far west of New South Wales and Queensland. Jeanie, without money and without friends, gladly accepted the offer of mother's help on a Diamantina station, and was packed off with what little luggage she had to the land of the great silence. No church bells, no cabs, no street hawkers shouting their wares — but a difference that had to be better. The only bell Jeanie heard for ever after was the station dinner gong which she had to beat to summon the hungry station hands to dinner.

Among the dashing young cavaliers of the big mustering camp — tall hats, heeled boots, jingling spurs — was a young coloured man. Always tidy, clean shaven, cheerful, fun loving — Raymond Forbes. Jeanie was ripe for romance. The boy (for he was only nineteen) was a king indeed when he rode — none better in the competitive cattle camp. Raymond could ride any horse that challenged the best saddle men in Kidman's employ. Raymond could outrun, outride, and sing better than most, and Jeanie loved him, loved him with all that her starved body and soul could give. She surrendered and was happy.

The young couple moved from station to station. Often short of food and of everything else, they lived on salt meat and damper for weeks at a time, and the price they paid was his health. Raymond developed the Barcoo Rot Scurvy and she knew that he was ill. All his laughter and cheerful hope and energy seemed to fade away.

Raymond had been born into a tribe of people far away to the west who, though scattered now, were his own folk, and it was to them he wanted to go for the sheltering acceptance of belonging. Down the dry Strzelecki Track Raymond and Jeanie went — she with a babe in arms, their only possessions a rattling buggy, two mules, a thin swag of blankets and a worn out canvas cover. On past the Moolawatana sandhills they went, enquiring all the time after his people until at Pralna they heard of a reserve that was being established for his people, and of a man in charge that would help them — somewhere to go.

This is the story of the scattered remnants of the Aboriginal tribes in this century — no houses, no huts, only a spring of water and hunting in the hills, but Raymond by this time was too ill to hunt and Jeanie was pregnant again. It has been

I ONCE MET A MAN . . .

the custom of peoples, tribes, to gather close together — probably a safety precaution, but the habit sticks. The Forbes lived close by the other remnants of the tribe — sharing, talking, a oneness that seemed comforting, until Raymond died. Then this young Londoner of English habits found herself without home, shelter, clothes, and however much others helped, she was alone.

Helpers erected a small one-room shelter made of cast away tins and boards; crude, scarcely better than a brush wurley. She chose to stay with her husband's people, those of her children's colour — her chosen place (she had no other). Intensely private, this English girl had no secret place — no toilet, no bathroom, no towels or soap — the poorest, loneliest woman on earth, charity unwanted and rejected. The two boys grew up belonging in the tribe and it seemed that Jean was content: the tribe became her people.

A famous writer, Ernestine Hall, passing through the area heard of the white English woman living alone (for she never married again) and tried to get close to Jeanie, to get a story, but Jeanie fled into the isolation of the bush. There are descendants now, and I wonder if they know about their grandmother.

Watching the pathetic figure of the tiny sunburnt woman carrying water from the common well, I used to wonder at the spirit so grand, so much bigger and heroic than any other, and could not help feeling pity until I learned that pity is an unnecessary word. Better to see the drama of Jeanie as creation at its best — hammering, shaping, melting humanity into something worthy of life.

I ONCE MET A MAN . . .

BILL GWYDER

Bill Gwyder wanted to be a drover. Some men serve five years as apprentice but Bill learned his trade with a hard teacher in a hard school in twenty-four weeks. Teacher was Martin Costello, in 1936. Bill must have learned fast and well because within three years the big stations such as Glengyle were trusting him with fat bullocks to rail to Marree, and in 1943 he made a trip that few men now living can claim; he took cattle from Kidman at the Finke River and drove them down the Macumba, behind the treacherous Lake Eyre bogs, to Oldfield's place at Mungeranie. His last trip was in 1968 but perhaps the one journey Bill would have remembered best was the crossing of the Cooper in flood, the year it went all the way to the lake, a once-in-a-lifetime happening. Although the Cooper has crossed the sandhills and spilled over into the Strzelecki three times that I can remember, it may not happen again until next century.

Some men live on the edge of civilisation, mingling a little with its hurrying people but not liking what they see, and themselves hurrying away to the peace of the places where no roads go by. Such men become drovers, stockmen in far places, cooks on lonely stations; some even forget to talk, or, if not, do not wish to speak much or often. Bill was like that: he could sing around the cattle on night watch, or abuse an erring mate: offered little of himself and expected less of others. A travelling man, but not a wandering man, he had a regular beat and for most of his droving life kept to it. At last he became known as a Birdsville track drover — quite a title if such is your ambition to become a top drover.

Even men like Bill whose life on the droving track earn them the envied accolade of "Boss Drover" have smashes. Some take delivery of a mob that contains a restless nucleus of rogues who will rush at the drop of a hat. Such cattle are singled out and watched but it does happen, and Bill has had his share of disastrous rushes where hundreds, although seldom complete mobs, go wildly into the night and are never collected.

Bill had one bad run of luck: he was moving a quiet mob

I ONCE MET A MAN . . .

when a wild storm, such as seldom, if ever before, rolled over him. The Lake Eyre district is a land of sandstorms, similar to the great and feared storms of the Sahara and Gobi Deserts. I sometimes wonder if the sandstorm that overwhelmed Bill Gwyder was the same storm that rolled over my hut a hundred miles further south. The bullocks walked before the wind: nothing could stop them. Bill put his packs together and pulled his campsheet over him and his boys. The fury of the first blast completed the dispersal of the cattle and they walked off into the darkness of a storm that screamed and blasted, howling like a banshee and as Bill explained briefly, "Scared the hell out of me." The sand buried the packs and if the drovers had not stirred would have buried and smothered them. Some of the packhorses and plant survived and were later collected at the bore head, but of the cattle nothing is known. It was a rare but certain wipe-out. No one blamed Bill: no one could. Nature in the desert can be cruel and desperately fierce.

I have good, very good, reason to remember that storm. After days of the blow, my wife announced that she had had enough.

Bill continued droving.

I ONCE MET A MAN . . .

TOM QUILTY

Why would the Irish sooner fight than eat, or the English feel it proper to look like gentlemen? Can a Chinaman help digging in the good earth, or a slave help dancing? Marx had it all worked out, but I reckon he was wrong.

Tom was Irish, and the code was right for him, nothing nasty about the fighting feeling, it was just there — just Irish. Great man, Tom. If he saw a young man who looked honest, he'd bet on it and give him a thousand bullocks on credit. There were two sides to the gift of course, there was a thousand fewer bullocks to feed, a sale was made and, bless him, he might have made a friend — often did. What he was had great importance to Tom — he was a cattleman and that was everything, or almost. Ability to drink rum, play the saw and write a verse had their place, but overshadowing all was his love for a woman.

She was a publican's daughter and being a drinking man Tom saw a lot of her and knew that he had to have her — now. Possession of her meant leaving all else — station, cattle, wife, family, and the land where all his young days were spent; he paid the price and put a thousand sheltering miles behind him. The couple, fleeing from the punishment of guilt by public verdict, sought the loneliest place in all the land, a piece of country that nobody wanted — crocodiles, bamboo — all the pests of the coastal plains.

He called it Coolibah. Together they tamed the wide land, brought outlaw cattle into branded herds, and when small tragedies struck they suffered together. Children came and at last prosperity — old sins became history. There was never a sense of guilt in leaving the Queensland side and setting up in the Kimberleys, only escape, and being busy taming a wilderness leaves no time for remorse.

We were drinking in the old bush pub at Hall's Creek, that is before the old town was shifted. Celebrating really, for as was our custom when the bullocks were ready for the road we put them into the horse paddock and proceeded to christen the event, akin to pouring a dram on the baby's head — an assurance of a safe trip. Strange, in all the years that we took Tom's bullocks there was never a crash, such as losing them in a night rush, or the big loss with pleuro or redwater.

Time came when the southern people wanted a patron for the latest fad — proving you could ride a hundred miles in a day. Tom had been doing that for most of his life, like sending a telegram, riding for help. It was a natural part of his life and it pleased him that a new generation wanted to try. Yes, he would give a thousand pounds to make a cup, and that's how it started — the Quilty Cup. That one was christened in the old pub, too.

BOBBY
AMOS

The wind blew through the Flinders Ranges, as cold as the polar seas where the south winds come from. We had broken down on a trip from the mission at Nepabunna and were going south. The bleak hills of the Flinders were no comfort, nothing grew there, not even edible grass and we knew all the native foods.

Bob had a cast in the eye that made him look formidable; trachoma and sandy blight took a heavy toll on the Aboriginals, and it was from such a camp that Bob came. Like most of his clan, he had been "rescued" from his mother's people and placed in a home from where he and all the saved were farmed out as servants, call it slaves if you will. A cheerful, willing boy, sort of a man Friday to me he was, and company too in those cheerless days when a boy trained in survival skills by his people was a big help in living off the land as we were. For those were depression days and Government handouts were not for me.

The wheel of the old truck flew off its axle and rolled away down the hill — stubb axle they told me later, but it could have been anything for all I knew. All we had (and little enough it was) we rolled up in our blankets, strapped them up and set off on foot. It was only thirty miles or so to the nearest rail town, but thirty dry miles. The sun came out later in the day — as is the case in the centre, the bitter cold of night can be a burning sun by noon. Bob trudged along carrying a swag almost as big as his starved little body: it must have been a tough camp where Bobby was born, probably on Neales Creek below Oodnadatta — the poorest of the last of the tribes were there on the Neales. By night we had come to see the lights of Beltana and there in the creek bed, without rations, we dug a shallow soak for water and camped all in.

Don't say that humping the bluey is romantic. Bush towns don't come alive too early, at least that one seemed to sleep on forever. As we watched the sun rise, the town showed some promise. Bob's eyes, never very clear, were running pus and his ragged clothes and dusty face were a match for mine. We looked what we were.

I ONCE MET A MAN . . .

Down the street came the local padre on his mission of Christian visits to the outback stations, driving a car. That to us was the symbol of affluence and with our perceptions having been sharpened by lack of two days' eating, we pulled him up. No doubt about his identity, with his white, roundabout clerical collar. I put the case, hoping that I sounded desperate, and Bobby certainly looked the part as a needy one. Padre looked us over and to my last day I shall hear his verdict: "We do not feed the likes of you."

The train carrying cattle pulled in just then and by night we were safely in the cells of the police station at Port Augusta, a hundred miles away. The beds in the cells are narrow and the food is not good but it's not charity. "Though I give my body to be burned, and have not charity . . ."

Where are you, Bobby? It's been a long time, but I remember.

SHE

$\mathbf{W}$hat! No great women? Of course, plenty of them. "Then," you ask, "what of them? Why not put their story on record?" Danger there, I see problems; nevertheless I shall begin and see what rocks and shoals lie there and, if possible, avoid creating any great waves.

I once met a man who had a family of five daughters, several families in fact. He was the poet type, probably over eighty when his daughter took me to meet him. He had the look of eagles, one who has soared to great heights and looked down on lesser men; a soldier of distinction, farmer, gun shearer; and for many years a fugitive from what he believed to be capitalist justice; a man of many names, many camp fires, many women, a traveller on the face of the earth, not beaten. The girl, it was his child, long estranged, loved him.

His crime, of which the law knows and which hearsay confirms, was never solved because the perpetrator was never caught. When the great shearers' strike of 1890-92 was on in Queensland and the powers that be sent a boatload of strike-

I ONCE MET A MAN . . .

breaking shearers up the Darling in a boat called the *Rodney*, Davenport, as he was then known, led a party of men aboard at the junction of the Darling with the Murray and sank the *Rodney*, overpowered the strike-breakers and escaped. That was in 1892. Now, over ninety years later, locals at Wentworth tell me that the *Rodney* will be raised and restored. Davenport is long since dead, his daughter is still alive.

Great events colour the life of those who take part. In this case, the fugitive from the wrath of the then strong squatters' law went into hiding and became a farmer in the isolated backblocks of the Murray Mallee. It was a time to be remembered with nostalgia by his five girl children — the ploughman coming home to nurse the little ones who might find a rabbit in Dad's pocket, sometimes a pretty stone, a bunch of wild flowers, always something.

This was one of Gray's men — "Some mute, inglorious Milton here may rest, some Cromwell guiltless of his country's blood." Some such unknown men beget great children: his daughters, reared in deep poverty when Davenport went off to war in 1914, were persons of dignity and character far above all others of any class or custom. Reared in many places, always on the run, never able to stay at one school long and so with little learning, and always the humbling of bare-foot poverty — the girl who introduced me to Davenport was her father's child, a poet in her own right who raised six children in the image of the father she loved; not as rebels, not as outcasts, as they well could be, for these also were raised in like circumstances. All had the style, the strength, the character that only good breeding can give: she was a great lady.

I married her.

I ONCE MET A MAN . . .

BILL
WADE

Wade worked for Schenk, a mission man at Mount Margaret, a goldfield town in Western Australia. Schenk was by his own standards a very religious man and no doubt wanted to "do good" by the blacks, and if clothing the blacks and breaking up their religion is seen to be good, then he succeeded. I suppose only after the great settlement, when all lives and intentions are assessed and we listen to the final judgment, then may we pass comment on the results of the work of such as Schenk. He baptised the whole tribe at Mount Margaret and as evidence that the message got through I am told that he later caught the people dunking the chooks in a tub. The black ones were supposed to represent Aboriginals, the brown the half-castes and the white chooks represented the whites. Quite symbolic but no laughs — that came later.

Some men get religious and change their habits, but stay the same at base. The mean ones stay mean but they talk differently. I never worked Schenk out but he had a way with him and certainly got some results with me the time I worked for him cutting wood and burning lime, walking five miles each way to the mulga stand to cut logs and raking gravel off the hill for concrete. Still I get a good feeling — like when his old wife, at eighty, wrote and told me that the tank had stood and served the people well and was still there. They never gave up on me for on her death bed, sixty-six years after she had last seen me, she implored me on a tape to give up my evil ways and join the march to glory. I still have the tape, it's a bit blurred by her wavering voice but it was apparently one of her last utterances. She will no doubt be pleading my case, but I have great belief in the mercy of the one she served.

One of the young apprentices at Schenk's place was called Wade — an Englishman and always telling of the sins he had committed as a sailor in every port, genuine but hard to take. Still, when Schenk offered him a job exploring the Gibson Desert area to see what lost souls there might be out there, Wade took me on as his camel boy. I was mighty pleased to have a big horizon ahead of me and hurried to Oodnadatta to buy some camels. The budget was very limited but I wanted seven camels, four boxes, five saddles for packs and two riding saddles, water canteens, guns and rifles, and food for a year — rice, flour, salt, baking powder, dried vegetables, tea, sugar and a few extras. The camels came first and then the ropes and bags for the packs; food came last. Later, time showed that this was a mistake. Still, I had the exuberance of youth and really believed we could live off the land. At least, I did — Wade believed in the loaves and fishes and the providers of manna.

We passed through station country on our way to the far west and the desert mountains — Lasseter's hills (but before his time) — the Petermann, Musgrave, Mann and Tompkinson

I ONCE MET A MAN . . .

Ranges. It was three hundred miles from Oodnadatta to where the ranges started. The stockmen that I fraternised with along the way were envious of the chance to meet the nude ladies of the wild tribes — they would risk a spear, they said. Wade couldn't stop me looking but he put strict limits on his conscience. He probably saved my life, for the wild boys were very good with spear and nulla.

It was another world: everything was new and exciting — learning to track, spear, throw a boomerang — I tried it all and soon managed a few words of the local dialect. Wade never tried to learn. He held the white man's view that we whites had all the secrets to heaven and most of the authority on earth. He was content to sing hymns and because he was such a very ordinary singer, I believed that the corroboree was better music. I would say that the only things he had going for him as far as communicating went were a nice smile and good intentions.

Wade was a good man showing a lot of evidence of a change of habits. On his own say-so, he had been an all-out, full-time splendid sinner. He was an awfully dull companion and we often went a week without words, but he had turned his back on sin. One thing he taught me was how to get out of trouble — if we were down in the Gibson and had little chance of finding water and small chance of getting back to water alive, he would have a long session with his boss — a bit one-sided I would say, but a full night of very earnest pleading on his knees under the stars always brought results. Evidence of course remains — I am still around.

In a strange coincidence, I have just read *My Place* by Sally Morgan — quite a book. Seems she married the grandson of Rod Schenk, the man referred to earlier in this yarn, the man I burned the lime with and built the tank for. Stranger still, in Sally's book she speaks about her travels to find her people and about Aboriginals who on meeting her demanded "Was she a Christian?" The evangelists who caused this revolution came from far away in the Warburton Ranges, no doubt some of Bill Wade's converts.

When I left Wade with his string of camels that had been my worry for long months in the Musgrave Ranges and deserts beyond, he went east from his old base at Laverton in the Western Australian goldfield. He pulled up in the Warburton Ranges, the loneliest place in Australia, married an Oodnadatta mission girl, Harris, and continued preaching to the tribes. Twice now I have heard of the fiery Aboriginal evangelists who are heading the tribes to Heaven by total conversion. Wade's work, no doubt.

JACKIE
CADELL

The story goes that Jackie was the son of a Malay man on Tom Liddle's place at Katherine in the Northern Territory, and that Jackie's mother was an Aboriginal. Fact is that Jackie is every bit Chinese in looks and character; things get a bit mixed sometimes but whatever the breed it does not matter because Jackie is a very special man.

Ted Low of Oodnadatta brought Jackie down to Adelaide in 1945 to ride in the first official rodeo that the Australian Rough Riders ever held. Ted was known as a top man among top men, and there is no higher classification; Ted reckoned that Jackie was the fastest leg and the prettiest rider ever to fork an outlaw horse, and to prove his point he brought Jackie to Adelaide to match him against Australia's best at the rodeo.

Two days after the rodeo the caretaker at the rodeo grounds called me on the phone and advised that there was an injured man lying in a shed at the grounds. "Seems like he has a broken shoulder." Sure enough, Jackie had been hurt and, without asking for help, had crawled into the shed (I suppose like a wounded dog would do) and there he lay. Jackie recovered and for fifteen years or more stayed with me as rider, groom and friend. His bride, Ethel, was very dark; the children, bright and intelligent, were raised in a small house at Northfield.

When the time came for Ethel to have her first child, they were living in a cottage in the Adelaide hills and Jackie came down every day to North Adelaide to look after my horses. I suggested that he should take thought now for Ethel being alone there in the hills. He thought and with his usual poker face and with expression of great confidence in his boss he replied, "That your business, Mr Williams." The saying became a catchcry among many employees for years.

Many years later Jackie, an old man, turned up at the 50th Anniversary of the Marrabel rodeo. As old friends celebrated, we were gathering about a table where Smoky Dawson, the Western singer, and I were signing his recently launched books, Smoky autographing the books as I helped with the honours. A gentle tap on my shoulder and there was Jackie, nice suit, polished boots, elegant as always. "You like my hautograph, Mr Williams?"

THE TWO JIMS

What is success? This question arises often along the way.
We all know the philosophies of the many who have defined
achievement, honour, fame, wealth, and all the attributes that
carry the definition of "success". Chances are that most folk
don't meet a lot of very successful men, who in turn don't
have the time or opportunity to share a crust with the very
poor.

Both the rich and the very poor have crossed my path
and among them a few who one could classify as successful.
The ownership or control of great wealth seldom denotes large
spending but rather power which allows luxury. Such may
have access to many bathrooms, but can use only one at a
time; many houses, which are an obligation rather than useful;
five cars, where one would do; fawning women, when happiness
with one is all.

Old Jim had none of these, not even a house. He did have
an old, kind mule that served to carry his groceries, and for
shelter a straw-thatched roof. Nor did he have a library, but
the people who came by knew he liked books and used the

lending of their favourite books as an excuse to call on him and talk about the books. Jim had, in his long life, read very widely and gained a depth of knowledge that most people envied. He was good with his hands and made odd things that callers liked to buy: a wooden chair; a carved emu egg; a plaited bridle; a carved wooden spoon; a special knife; a tiny wind-blown forge, where he melted down odd metals. He talked with pleasure about melting down gold from fine dust for a prospector. Jim was never in a hurry for, when the mood took him, he would walk in the bush and find pieces of wood for raw material, or read a book, or whittle a stick. Young people sat on his bench and told him their troubles, talked about the future, even how they might become rich, for he knew how people made money. He himself advised against the race for riches. Jim no doubt was a very successful man.

Because I have walked the corridors of power and trod on the deep carpets of the very rich, it has been my opportunity to take stock of what effect possessions have on men and women. A few, very few, are successful by the standards time has taught me. I could tell tales of many rich people who are not successful. It will suffice to write of one who is.

James started life as a message boy. I will not tell you where because that would nominate him at once and that is not my intention. As a message boy he read the messages and he tells, with some pride, that often he profited by the news that passed between the captains of industry: trade secrets; stock exchange tips; deals of great moment. Soon his enterprise and cheer led him slowly up the ladder, gaining momentum as he went — from better job to bigger responsibility. He studied accounting and law on the way. At last he reached the top and from there many times I asked him, "Where now?"

He bought the largest house, the finest land, moved in the best circles, housed the most beautiful girls, and then? And then the façade, the gilt of being someone faded and he looked back at the path by which he had climbed, and thought about who, if any, were happy among his elevated friends.

Jim closed the chapter, put away the running shoes, closed the gate and retired into the solitude of books, the pleasure of sharing the great minds of the past, and he tended a garden.

Such is success.

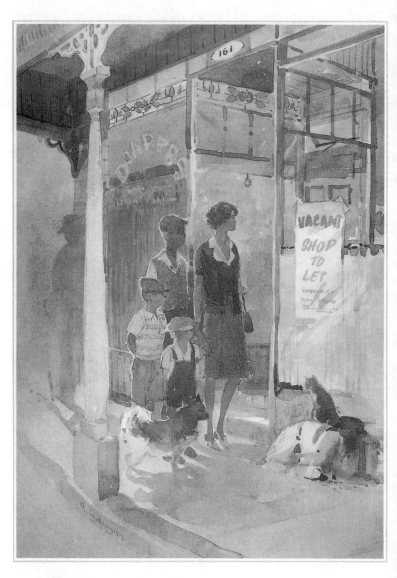

I ONCE MET A MAN . . .

EVE

If I might quote Kipling without taking a line out of context, he said, "The Colonel's Lady an' Judy O'Grady are sisters under their skins." In a very deep and investigative way it has often been my intent to research the question of the universality of the nature of the female of our species and it did occur to me to co-opt a woman or women to help my scientific intent. The hopelessness of the search for truth in the matter soon became apparent because of the closely kept secrets held in a subconscious defence by females since the time of Eve. To illustrate the evidence of the freemasonry of women let me give some examples.

I remember Peggy, she was a frail little thing, seemed too little to have children — narrow in the hips, thin legs, no bust at all. Everybody liked little Peggy. Like a little cheerful bird she was, but would she ever marry, and if she did, what then?

It was a surprise when Tom came along. Big strapping lad he was — thick legs, bulging muscles, neck like a bull.

Tom courted dainty Peg and the frail slip of a girl was married to the giant, football-playing strongman, Tom.

Peggy was soon pregnant, and from nowhere at all Peg had a son, a big baby too, number one . . . number two . . . number three. Peg had three strapping sons, and by now nobody questioned miracles — the size of women is deceptive.

Apparently since time began women have known all these things about them being superior but have not wanted the secret revealed, preferring to look admiringly into a man's eyes, declaring his sovereignty, thus allowing vanity to keep him in thraldom.

> Know this and be content,
> Deny it to your peril.

As happens sometimes to powerful men, Tom developed a muscular rheumatism; in a few years he was doubled up with pains and ceased altogether to carry the burden of a growing family. The boys were still at school and needed care. Tom needed all kinds of help. Out of frail little Peggy we saw the giant spirit of independence emerge. She rented a shop and, with a power that only great spirits have, won the hearts and custom of custom. "Success is to serve," and around the clock wee Peggy served on to success — a success that was security for Tom and the boys again.

The female of the species is stronger than the male.

She was a Lady married to a Knight of the realm, the toast of the party and, by virtue of personality, presided wherever her presence occasioned. The party was one of those old fashioned do's where every landholder of prestigious estates tried to outdo the other. It was many years ago now, so many

that I trust all the principal participants are either too old to remember or have left the scene. There was a yearly round of Polo, where the occasion demanded that all players at least had invitations to stay with either a chosen friend of the area or at an invited house. My annual host's house had, by reason of our mutual drinking abilities, become my habitual stopping-place without asking.

If, by reason of a heavy night, my host and I were not ready for the sideboard breakfast — where special morning dress was the custom — then we were excused by the hostess as being off colour as usual. I would have thought she would have confided to other hostesses — in other words that we were not proletariat but rather more to-be-tolerated social drunks. If the day progressed to a recovery, then the family heirloom — Greener guns, long ago presented to the family by King Edward — would be unwrapped and the two recovered-from-hangover players would go quail shooting and take a long walk in preparation for the coming night's replay of the previous night. This elevation from my plebeian status had a marvellous effect on my progress toward respectability, and also it was rumoured that my latest house was a castle — silver-towered and all — and that I was believed to be the latest mining magnate.

Now to the point of the story: the nights had been a succession of who would survive the longest in an upstanding condition, to see the evening out or be last to leave — my host and I held that dubious honour. This night had progressed to the stage where those who could dance and those who had never learned to dance all mingled on the late-hour dance floor, and my partner chanced (or was it chance?) to be the titled lady. I fancy she was in no condition to take umbrage at my unsteady and untutored steps but with words that still

ring in my memory even now she said very softly, "I think you are a philistine."

Women are more perceptive than men.

Then there's the case of Lily, married to a successful publican. Lily claimed that she had an agreement with Jack that they would never interfere with each other's private lives. I would say that this was a foolish pact, for Jack went his own way under licence and Lily pretended to do likewise — but for reasons best known to womankind the pretence was an illusion because the flirting and make-believe of availability by Lily were a sham. The question arises why? My conclusion in this case is that women are more moral than men.

Another case to enliven the debate — the girl Eva — had good looks, a splendid body, charm and a quality of erudition beyond average (if there ever was an average).

Quite early, Eva learned the advantages of seduction and the leverage it gave her with males. Hers was a butterfly life, seemingly without need for any serious ties or attachments, and again, looking on as an interested party, I believed that Eva was getting away with the game successfully. Time came as time does and Eva, looking one day in the mirror (or so she told me), saw a wrinkle. By now her lifestyle was a widely known, unkept secret, for men do talk. Eva had been looking long and regularly for the man who would be a steady partner to settle down with. The one she chose was not as good as some that she had but was a regular fellow, although a bit dull. Eva decided that she could not live with her past unless she told Fred the truth of her wanderings and so in the cause of absolute confession laid her black soul bare. Fred married her but exchanged no confidences.

Time went by and inevitably the stress of togetherness precipitated a first and all-out quarrel. It was over a trifling matter, Eva's spending habits — or was it trifling? The story of her infidelities, so dutifully confided by Eva, was shouted as evidence of her unsuitability to be his, Fred's, wife. Fred had never told Eva his side of the coin — but I knew it.

It would seem that women are more truthful than men.

FANNY

The people who emerged from the newly industrialised England spread over the British Empire as escapees, or that is how I see them, leaving the horrors of England, Ireland, Wales, and Scotland to make a new world, bringing with them Victorianism plus Calvinism, even though some may have been convicts.

In the early 1900s, Victorian ideas were still strong, dominating politics and social behaviour, with strong influence on law and public morality.

This present age could be called the age of revolution: Women's Lib, Russian reconstruction, China convolutions, half the world rebelling with the other half restless. This has been my era, nine years old when Lenin led the 1917 revolt, the suffragettes already parading; forty-one years old when the Chinese followed Russia. Two wars in that time.

Fanny Mitchell was born in the early 1880s with all the weights of Victorianism on her young mind and constraints that were not lessened after a century of change. She saw

it all, and lived into the 1980s, through the electronic revolution that put horse transport off the roads, changed life from kerosene lanterns to a world lit by incandescent globes.

Did all this change Fanny Mitchell after living through all this that was new for the first time in history? Not at all, Fanny kept to the even tenor of her ways, doubting still that women had rights to raise their voices (or their skirts). Perhaps the strongest conviction of Victorian women concerned the wrong that followed the exposure of the female figure. Some say that we are what heredity or environment make us. I think Marx forgot to take into account the ethics of the subject's time for, without doubt, the great religious revivals of the nineteenth century moulded that era.

I can think of many prominent men living now who still show the causations that moulded Fanny. With all the straitjacket of the era in which Fanny lived and died there are other freedoms of the mind and spirit worth noting.

She could look at the darkening sky as a storm filled the west with lightning and crashes of thunder holding our young hands, the while looking out the window with the light of wonder and somehow revelling in the crashing storm. Sweet garden scents were paradise to Fanny: the breath of the Eucalypts, the perfume of the lilac, all nature was somehow God's garden.

The rolling rippling wheat fields waving in the wind were ecstasy to a woman born to love the ripening field. She would stand in awe of the grandeur of fields coming alive in spring and somehow transfer this wonderment to us, her children. These freedoms of the spirit perhaps balance the other bindings of tradition. Fanny, my mother.

DR AITKEN

Doctors of the early years, before 1912, that is, general practitioners of the country towns, were horse and buggy men. Messengers rode desperately across country to tell of their sick or dying, and doctors harnessed the finest team in the land to drive night and day to respond to the urgent need. Doctors were the best market for the finest animals to be offered and Dr Aitken was typical of the great physicians who laid their own life on the line day by day to keep faith. His were the very best horses to be got — he *must* be there quickly.

My mother was very sparing in her prayer for mankind in general, but Dr Aitken, the old Scottish medico, was her hero. She quoted him at every opportunity: "If Epsom salts was a guinea an ounce it would be cheap at the price." Seems like she could stretch her puritanical standards in his case, for it was well known that when someone had urgent need for help: a broken leg, an acute appendix, a woman in labour far out in the bush where bad roads, or no roads, made those wild racing dashes to help a daily adventure, Aitken never refused, never failed.

My mother tells the story that the station master, of Italian blood, a fierce-visaged man who held his position as chief very seriously, sired a brilliant son who early in his scholastic days showed promise and came to the notice of Dr Aitken. Station masters with big families could not afford university for their sons. This Aitken knew, and in due course, it was he who suggested that the brilliant child be his protégé and become a doctor. How well he judged, for the child, the youth, the man became a famous physician long after Aitken died — Sir Raphael Cilento.

I ONCE MET A MAN . . .

GYPSY
SMITH

Awareness of charlatans comes with experience, at least to some folk, but the fooling of people goes on from generation to new generation — not always about money, more often about power or persuasion. It is about persuasion that this story is concerned. Shame on me if I cast doubt about one, or all, of the many religious persuasions in this world, nor would I point a finger at crusaders at large, but there are some bad apples in the barrel. Alternatively there must be some good ones.

Although I have not gone out of my way to listen to many preachers, there does come to mind one such who left a lasting impression on my young, searching mind — though I admit that, at the time I was in a very susceptible state and was an impressionable age. Walking down one of the more disreputable streets of a big city, lately having come from an area where girls were more scattered than the big cattle stations, I was impressed to see a group of interesting girls of about my age, clustered around a tiny organ. A preacher

I ONCE MET A MAN . . .

was telling anybody who would listen about their sins, which they did not want to know about. The preacher wouldn't have stopped me but the girls looked interesting — they looked clean and tidy, and had something of the look of angels, for that was what the old Mohammedan priest at Marree described heaven as being like, full of good looking girls. One of these came handing out sheets of how-to-be-saved material and she stopped my way a bit longer than with the drunks and hard cases lounging about. Now, I had never thought of myself as being good looking, but she was very special so that I decided that lingering a bit longer might be better than wandering, and when they closed down the show I followed.

Headquarters was a dingy looking building between a broken-down factory and small tenement quarter. Next move was an invitation to go along to the old Exhibition building where one of the famous crusaders of England was preaching. With him was a man with a trumpet leading all the faithful in singing new songs; the atmosphere was full of exciting noise and to this day, sixty-five years later, I remember the tunes.

The man preaching was called Gypsy Smith — he looked like a full-time con man gypsy too, but his story was good. He had given up telling fortunes and pinching wallets, and claimed that by accepting Jesus's offer of life after death (not Mohammed's sort) he was born again into a new life. He sounded genuine and the music was terrific — I kept up the connection and married the girl, the best thing I ever did.

ALAN BENNETT
ROUGH RIDER

The story I have to tell is no secret, nor does it bring shame to the actors in the drama.

For forty years Alan Bennett and I had been friends, me sharing his problems, he sharing mine. There would be none who would question that he was the most durable, aggressive rider in the Australian Rodeo circuit. His first contest was also the first official rodeo of the Australian Rough Riders' Association — 1945 — and for thirty years or more his passing by was marked by broken noses and split lips, often his own. Once he felt the need to have his face rebuilt but the beauty lasted less than six months, for the man had not changed.

My boys and I were cutting posts and clearing fencelines at Rockybar when Alan called. His swag was in the back of the vehicle and, strangely out of character, he joined the gang. Something was wrong. First chance I asked, not probing, just a passing question and he told me. "Should have married that girl!"

This was a mighty determined statement from a man who has weathered the wiles of hopefuls from a hundred towns and cities, for girls admired a hero rider who looked all man. "That girl" was a New Zealand redhead and pretty, who had done the northern rodeo circuit and gone on to Sydney, en route for home.

"I'll be best man, Alan. You'll catch her in Sydney and I know a priest who will tie you up. Let's go."

To marry is a beginning, to stay married is a heaven-sent gift and heaven owed Alan nothing; within the year Evelyn was back in New Zealand. Alan followed. A child was born and, with his whole heart to give him his due, Alan tried to break the stubborn girl's resolve to end the marriage. Alan stayed and fretted and did what all repentant husbands do. To no avail — she would not give in nor would she let him have the child, his child. All his riding, fighting ambitions were pale compared to his wish to have Shane, his boy.

I had a ring on the phone from New Zealand. Would I take and hide and raise the child if he could abduct his son? The plea was almost a sob. Coming from such a powerful angry man, I felt for him, he was my friend and she was not.

"Yes, Alan."

Nineteen years went by and before me stood two visitors, a redheaded woman and a young man, the dead spit of Alan Bennett. She had learned of the conspiracy and had kept her son, and now she was defiant. "I did better than you would have!" The words were stark but not angry. Excusing myself I rushed to an inside phone and rang Alan Bennett in Perth. "Alan, Shane is here."

Alan came — that was years ago. Alan's days are numbered now, but last week he passed by and stayed a while — Shane was with him.

I ONCE MET A MAN . . .

B O B
THE COMMO

In the days when free speech was part of the rights that everybody believed were theirs, there was a Sunday habit of Adelaide folk to gather in the Botanic Gardens and listen to revolutionary speeches like the Salvation Army who sang "Onward Christian Soldiers" and believed in it. There were others who pleaded to allow Henry George's Single Tax a chance; a few loners advertising; a Labor ring, well supported; never of course a Liberal candidate — the park was for those who believed in change.

Every Sunday one lone man mounted a box without fanfare to proclaim the gospel of a new world: only five years before the Russians had announced their intention of building the new world which Bob believed in.

Most young men believe that they know better than their elders, particularly better than the prosperous looking leaders of Government. Not many girls went public in those early twenties though; it was not done, the age of equality was not yet.

I must confess to sympathy with the toiling masses of the

world who were avidly repeating the Marxian slogan: "The workers have nothing to lose but their chains . . . Workers of the world unite."

The lone voice of Bob, the communist, was such to attract young people lately suffering from the heavy hand of Mr Keynes, the English banker who led the world into a decade of dark depression. Even now Keynes has his disciples who are fool enough to believe that a rod for the workers' back is good for society.

Having nothing to do but complain, I found Bob saying just the right things to enlighten my eager mind; but his bold, fearsome attitude had an aura of the complete outsider, so foreign to my upbringing in a conservative family that it made it very hard for me to even speak to the evangel of change. Noting my several attendances to his speech among a small audience, Bob took time off the stump to hand me a booklet on Marx's theory of surplus profit.

The obviously poor working man must have found valuable booklets expensive for his small budget, for Bob was a casual labourer. The booklet had a doctrine concerning the weakness of capitalism, proclaiming that wages never equalled the price of goods and services produced by that labour. The theory was that profit on labour, plus interest on capital, never reached the worker as purchaser of goods and services produced by that labour. I have pondered this equation for sixty years or more without reaching a conclusion but at that time Bob's message seemed simple sense.

Bob was a little older than me but not enough to make the difference that I could not talk to him, with the result that he became a regular visitor to our house. I liked Bob, he was a simple sincere man who believed everything he preached about the plight of workers, but of course he did not then know about the great discovery that the capital controllers of the world had made. They had hit on a brilliant solution to the difference between the cost of goods and purchasing power — inflation by four per cent. Brilliant indeed, and it saved capitalism. A pity Bob is not around now to see the ultimate result of inflation which for sixty years has breached the gap between workers' wages and the cost of goods.

Bob urged me to join his crusade to save the toiling masses of the world from capitalism. I had a family, rent to pay, a way to make in life which brooked no delay, such as taking time off to change the system. I told Bob how cowardly I felt, how selfish my motives were for not joining the revolution that he was sure would come within ten years. I could not wait that long, the price was too high: better to join the then rulers, the powers that be, the system, however evil it might be. We drifted apart, Bob and I: he to enlarge his hate and fight for a change that never came, while I joined the system which, however wrong, still works. I still pay tribute to those brave souls who leave their life's blood in the arena of great endeavour, never knowing at the last whether they were right, but die believing.

MIKE

Mike was born of very humble parents, without, what is called, a "start in life". He always kept his head up and, what is more, helped keep mine out of the mire through the tough depression years. There was no physical reason why others should look up to him but I did. Mike had no money, position, or power, just an aristocracy of character.

Throughout a long life, Mike has been close to me. Every time I deviated, weakened, or lost my way, he has been there to help. No feeble hand or dull reformer could have kept me on the straight and narrow during the great depression of the thirties. Mike was a Mason and that might have helped, but I never heard him say a pious word, or protest, even though he knew I was wrong. Even when, as a rebel, I was jailed for vagrancy, Mike only laughed with me, or when my ethics did not match his own there was no lecture.

When my world collapsed, when an overburdened mind blanked out, Mike picked up the load, sent me money, paid the bills, handing back the reins when I was ready, without a word. When there was an overload and he thought that

it might become too much for me, Mike bought me a ticket to India, telling me to stay there among the poor people until their poverty and need showed the way to my own fortunate life. This medicine worked. It took a year, perhaps more, but that was the turning point in a too busy life gone sour, which now I see that Dr Mike foresaw, and predictably set me right. That was the work of a very wise man.

Not many people ever reach that spiritual level of benevolence where they can forgive others their weaknesses, hold out the hand of friendship without any condemnation.

There have been times when mistakes could have been called crimes — such errors lie buried in the memory of a faithful heart, without any care that judgment would be called. All the darkest secrets of my life are in good custody.

In 1953 the call of life, other than the desk and telephone, was strong on me, but how could a complex "machine" be abandoned? Mike did not ask for power of attorney which he could have had, just an agreement by word was all with which he bade me go. That was thirty-five years ago, during which long years Mike kept trust even when I never went back to support him. It is a strong man indeed that needs no support . . .

GORDON
BILLINGS

Let's not say the hard times should come often, but they do breed a certain kind of determined man. Gordon grew to full height about that time, which happened to coincide with my looking for a sturdy mate. I had served my time as a junior assistant with camels, under a wandering master, long enough to see country where no settlers had taken up land, quite unexploited, country with wild life — human and fauna — still enjoying that benefit.

Empty land and opportunity in the Musgrave and Petermann Ranges looked promising to me to make a possible fortune in dingo scalps. All I needed was a string of camels and a mate; Gordon could provide both. We went west from Oodnadatta well equipped to trade with the tribes for scalps, also with a contract from the South Australian Museum to catch and preserve a bilby (a rare white-tailed, nocturnal, pouched, rabbit-type animal), the night parrot, migratory birds, plus insects. For preparation of these birds and mammals, the curator of the museum gave us a crash course in skinning, scraping and painting the bodies with formalin. All this work made it necessary to have tanks for liquids, boxes for specimens and jars for reptiles. Packing such equipment on camels is not easy, nor is it safe to reckon on the percentage of survival. The first camel to buck off a load carried jars that leaked most of the formalin, putting an end to our prospects for fortune. The insects brought the princely price of twopence each — had we known this in advance we would have brought back everything that came to the lantern at night. We did get a few rare specimens but the scalp business paid our way.

The Musgraves and the Mann Ranges have a unique way of starting without hills first, clean off the plain, rising to great rocky heights. Our technique was to drag a trail around the foot of the mountain where the dogs had a track leading to water, brushing the ground to leave a soft place to show tracks. Gordon and I would listen to the whispering voices of the still night, faint night sounds — far-away mating calls, night birds' wings rustling the evening air, crickets calling their constant whirring in the night. We would listen past these for more likely noises — a spearman, a dog howling to the rising moon. One must be alone to fully appreciate the lonely places, the desert wind, the quiet where nothing intrudes.

Gordon liked to walk quietly out into the night and sit in a lonely place, listening. He feared the tribesmen more than I, because experience had told me that spearmen do not usually travel in the night. Although there had been one night, a year before, when Wade and I were camped at Days Gully in the Mann Ranges when our camp, protected by a deep circle of leaves, had been probed by some inquisitive young men who stole every movable article outside the leaf, and that in the dead of night.

Gordon's brother Alec was Pentecostal — speaking tongues

and all that, always crusading. Gordon seemed to take to my cathedral of the open range, the high mountains, the soft wind and quiet of the night as reverence for the Creator. We were satisfied with our special communion with the God of all natures, worshipped at this altar, and found forgiveness. What conceited arrogance to confine worship to within church walls.

This attitude of quietness of spirit in Gordon was very companionable, quite different to the fierce praying and professing of my missionary boss of the previous years, even though he did seem to get results. No doubt heaven will have to be very compartmentalised.

There are times in desert travel when the unexpected produces stress that brings out the best and the worst in men — sand storms, long stretches without water, sickness. There are no sheltering walls for the traveller, no guidance for the lost, or doctors to give comfort. At times, on this journey with Billings, we would be five hundred walking miles from anywhere when I discovered what a very special kind of durable man he was.

After months of travel we were well cashed up, having sold our scalps to the depot in Oodnadatta when, for want of a better offer, Gordon took a job with the railway, shovelling coal to the tenders on the rail engines. The norm was ten ton per man per day, and if that sounds like a lot of coal, it was.

In the half century since those days, I lost sight of my travelling mate but have no doubt his apprenticeship in the desert prepared him well for whatever way he went.

I ONCE MET·A MAN . . .

JIM PRINCE

orty years ago I was partner with Al MacDonald, a part-Maori. We had several mines going within a hundred miles of Tennant Creek and one of these mines was at Mosquito Creek, about twenty miles east of the highway, out towards the Simpson Desert. Miners work long hours, that is, if they have a share in the mine.

The day closed off at sundown in the camp at Mosquito Creek and when the engines driving the separation table supervised by old Jim stopped, he in turn shut off the water on the Wiffley separation table and beckoned me to follow him. We were sharing spoils with Al MacDonald and he had control. The last operation in a wolfram mine such as ours is the separation table that puts the good ore into the bag. We had a shed full of bags and it was almost time to celebrate — about ten thousand pounds worth of the black and white ore was locked up that night. Jim led me to his tent and, closing the flap of the tent, he pulled out a sugar bag from under his bed and tipped out the contents. It was quartz laced with pure gold, the best I had ever seen (and I had worked the nob when it went to five hundred ounces to the ton).

Jim looked at me carefully, trying to look deeper than the camera would show. Could he trust me? I read that in his long hard look. At last he spoke. "What do you think of it?" "It's good, Jim, very good, but this didn't come from here or anywhere near here." I had mined this area for a hundred miles north and south and knew the local rocks. Jim knew the question before I asked it and said quietly, "The Petermanns."

The Petermann Ranges stretch across the Western Australian border from the Territory, a very long walk from Tennant Creek. Deep in that jumble of rough hills is the Depot Glen where old Bob Buck hoisted the bones of Lasseter. Jim knew that I had looked that country over very well as a camel boy in 1926.

I questioned Jim about his waters and the lay of the hills to see if he really had been around the Petermanns by camel and he answered every query well — he had been there. Looking down at his crippled foot, I said, "You were game to ride a camel into that country." Jim couldn't walk back; that's what killed Lasseter.

I knew the Lasseter country well, as I had spent a lot of time there. The story old Ion Idriess put together on Lasseter is the kind of yarn that Ion is famous for. He was a past master of romance but, in his own words, *"The Desert Column* is the only real book I have to be proud of because it's my own history." When I told him about my years out in Lasseter country, before that old chap Lasseter took his last walkabout, Ion laughed and admitted that the tale he told was a mock up of his own about what *might* have happened. I do not believe that Jim Prince or any other prospector who followed the trail into the desolate Petermanns would have held too much

faith in Ion's book, but all prospectors live in hope and are not too hard to inspire with dreams of a golden mountain.

Jim was adamant. "No, I won't go out with camels again although I know that you still have a team ready to go." Jim knew that I had camels ready for just such a trip. "Get me a plane," Jim said, "and we will land on a salt lake near the gold." I took the bag of gold and headed off to Alice Springs were Kurt Johanssen, the son of an old friend, had a plane. Kurt refused to go and in some haste I went to Melbourne where my brother-in-law lived to discuss hiring a plane with him.

In my absence, Kurt somehow got old Jim Prince to let him fly him to the Petermanns — the story is history now. They crash-landed on the salt lake and busted a piece off the propeller, but Kurt was a genius for he rigged a pair of old cans into a condenser to get pure water from the salty dregs of the lake, told Jim to camp there and left him what food he had. With his knife, Kurt then whittled the broken wooden propeller to as even a balance as he could and took off. He made it back to a station and eventually got to Alice Springs. It took some time to arrange a new propeller and in the meantime Jim survived on the edge of the lake, not daring to go looking for gold because the country always looks different to the way you remember it and Jim had not been able to locate the reef from the air.

From his experience, Kurt now knew where the soft spots were on the lake bed and, true to his word, he rescued Jim Prince. Later, Jim Prince disappeared from the mining camp and try as we might we could find no trace of him; with him went the only real evidence that there is gold in the Lasseter country. Some day I plan to look, but it's getting late and camels are so slow and vehicles are not reliable, it's a big rough country.

Only lately I met an old mate — the one who tossed a coin to see whether it would be he or I who flew with Jim Prince to find his mountain of gold. We laughed together about the fact that neither of us was the one to be on the plane that crashed or perhaps one that never came back. And we laughed, too, about the clash we had with the law in our adventures at the beginning of the great gold mine Nobles Nob — but that's another story.

I ONCE MET A MAN . . .

AL MacDONALD

P art-Maori, one time sailor, sideshow fighter (for want of
a better job) — good at it too. Al travelled the Australian
shows as a boxer with an old time professional, one of John's
Boxing Troupe who would fight anybody for four rounds and
give ten pounds to the local who could beat the travelling
boys.

Al drifted to central Australia, built the regulation tin shack
at Tennant Creek where he married Mary. We called her
"Bloody Mary" for two reasons: firstly because, I being an
often welcome caller, Mary was instructed to feed the bloody
man; secondly because her simple technique of feeding the
man was to throw a fresh steak on the top of the wood stove
where its juice boiled over the sides of the hot top. Mary
would then slap the rare steak, together with a bottle of beer,
down in front of me: I was fed, excellent way of doing the
honours, slightly bloody.

Al and I were partners first at Mosquito Creek, where we
mined wolfram, calling ourselves the Falcon Gold Mining
Company until we went broke. Old Jim Prince, the man who

justly claimed to have found Lasseter's Reef, was our table operator handling the Wiffley separation table with skill. Old Jim showed me a room full of wolfram one night before displaying a bag full of rich gold specimens; the room full of wolfram disappeared soon after, but of course heavy bags can't walk away.

Years after, Al offered me a split in another wolfram show — I thought better of it. We mined the Black Angel and the White Devil mines together without any luck, although others went deeper and made big money on those leases. Our partnership had one great advantage for me, being a lesser, much inferior brawler when trouble erupted as trouble does in The Tennant and other goldfields pubs. Al's reputation was a sheltering wing. Al took considerable pride in drinking with, and mothering, the boss of the Nobles Nob, as was one of the dubious titles I held at that time.

Al and I had some success in floating winners on the stock exchange. At such times, Al would shed his dirty shearer's singlet, put on his sharkskin suit, hang the gold watch chain across his ample belly and drive up to the stock exchange in the elegant Packard, displaying all the trappings of a magnate miner. Al could play many parts.

Mary had two sons, good boys by Al's reckoning for his measure of progress in their education was based on who among the town's boys his sons could belt up, on equal or unequal terms. Mary had a problem and confided in me. "S'pose they die, them not yet christened?" I agreed that the situation was critical, with Al not having feelings about what could happen to a child without the blessing of the church. We also agreed that a little diplomacy on my part was needed: thus the plot was set. I would trade a christening for a few shares more in a new float we were scheming. It worked. A phone call

to Brother Mogg at the Christian Brothers School in Adelaide got results: Brother Mogg would take two heathen children to a Christian christening with assurance from me that the college would be endowed to the tune of a scholarship to enable one bush boy to be educated each year, giving me a foothold should I have to meet St Peter before my own graduation. The boys were christened; good men they are too, with the final payment yet to be called for by St Peter.

  I ONCE MET A MAN . . .

C E C I L
AND THE STOLEN GOLD

Perhaps it might be safe to tell this story now, although the men of the underworld have long memories. The chief actors would be old men now, but is it ever too late for retribution?

The gold mine of which my brother-in-law and I were the chief operators was booming — Nobles Nob — legend has it now as the richest hole in mining history. Threepenny shares doubled and trebled and doubled again until they peaked at fifteen pounds, making many millionaires. One pocket of ore that we struck at two hundred feet crushed five hundred ounces to the ton.

Men stayed down the mine at change of shifts, filling sugar bags with the stuff from this jeweller's shop of fabulous ore to be lifted out of the ventilator shaft in the night. Secret smelting plants developed in hidden mine shafts, stolen gold turned up everywhere — we knew about it. At one stage I sent a private arm to stop a train on a lonely Western Australian line to intercept a known carrier — the battle between the rich and the would-be-rich went on day and night. I did not begrudge the ox that trod out the corn his piece of the action but the ox got greedier as time went on. Spies would tell me of gold bars hidden in refrigerators: on trains and trucks at least one such informer died in the battle, his body found floating in a dam after he had been seen talking to me.

The war went on and it looked like a lost battle. When the extraction plant was in early days, we had an old fashioned amalgamation plant where the impregnated slurry passed over a mercury-lined plate. The boys would secrete the amalgam away in small lots; the loss was not too great. My reaction was to purchase locked grinding pans where the mercury was amalgamated with gold in a large steel vessel and the ore, when ground fine, lodged its gold as amalgamation with mercury to be recovered at given times by men in rubber boots. Some adventurous types would fill their rubber boots with the soft amalgam as part of their share in the growing wealth — these prospered mightily.

Our extracting plant expanded. We grew to the point where a multi-million cyanide extraction plant superseded the grinding pans. At great risk, the gang solved the problem of the dangerous, deadly cyanide solution, impregnated with gold, by syphoning off drums of the pregnant gold solution and precipitated it in small hidden plants, secreted in lonely mine shafts, with the help of also-stolen zinc fillings and other filters, plus manganese from the store. The barrels of poison cyanide solution were turned into bricks of solid gold — truly a big advance for the syndicate who shared the wealth.

My job — first locate the hidden plant and name the extractors, a game their side played for keeps. Al MacDonald, the acknowledged king-hit man of the Territory, was my

partner in several gold and wolfram mines. He kept me informed but Al himself lived on the edge of the dubious and perhaps darker side of the bright sunlight of ultimate respectability. He could only advise me without joining any hunt.

My son-in-law, recently a merchant-navy man, with a reputation for being better than most with his fists, offered to join me in the search for the gold thieves. The plan was that he would take a job as a miner on the understanding that he got into no fights. As Al MacDonald was not in the scheme, he let me know that Cec, my boy, was something of a soft sort, everybody in the mine seemed to kick him about. How little did they know how close they were to getting their ears boxed off! Cecil knew all the dirty tricks of barroom brawling and he was good at it. Cec joined the gang.

Word came for me to be in the Tennant Creek pub on a certain date at a given time. I was there sitting at the table in the lounge when Cec came in with his mate, carrying a parcel wrapped in newspaper. We ordered beers while Cec mentioned casually that they had a parcel to sell. My question: "How much?" The price was not high; I questioned the quality of the merchandise which seemed to offend the carrier of genuine Nobles Nob gold. He produced a chisel and with some trouble managed to cut a corner off the soft gold bar — it was a sizeable sample. I carried it with me for years.

I arrived back in Adelaide with the story and the sample and I can see Wilson, the Chairman of Directors, now musing in his quiet way. "Don't tell that story, lad," he said. "It could make you an accomplice. Where is Cec now?"

"The gang woke up to the plan that night," I said, "and we were gone in the morning before I could give them the money. I tipped off the police in Darwin and they did get a bar but it was not the bar with the corner missing."

The morning after the drama in the bar, Cec and I were aware that the sellers and the buyer would not meet for the seller had been alerted, but time had not allowed for the spy to be eliminated. We knew that there were no spare hours before something would be done to shut Cecil up permanently. We caught the plane together, leaving no name for Cec that he could be traced. Not many of the thieves were caught; they got their share but we made them earn it.

No hard feelings, boys, if you read this. Cecil is captain of an ocean-going vessel now — he will be hard to track.

F R A N K
THE NAVY MAN

The Australian navy was on patrol in the Mediterranean when the German army drove the allied forces out of Crete. A few escaped in open boats, among them my sister, Effie, a nurse with the Australian army. By a miracle, a destroyer, of which Frank was Navigating Officer, sighted the small rowboat with its survivors, and took them to Alexandria in Egypt where my sister joined the English hospital. It was thus that Frank became close to our family, an association that stayed strong for life.

Frank was a loyal sort of man, tough too; the navy breeds men that way. He had joined the navy on the deck, the only way possible for a man without backing, taking years to make the bridge. But he made it, mighty bitter that others could start at the top. Phyl waited patiently at home through the long, lonely years, while Frank climbed the ladder — not liking it, but she knew about the demon that drove a man who must. She had all the graces and virtues of a patient wife; waiting, always waiting for Frank to come home.

It must have hurt Frank to leave the navy after his long

battle to arrive at the top, but he did it for Phyl, started a new life as General Manager for my outfit in Adelaide. He was a good friend — took over my load, running many enterprises, and from then on mothered me through many bad years and unhappy times. No man ever had a truer mate.

I knew of the scars that those earlier lonely years had left on Phyl, but Frank never spoke about it, just tried to make it up, give back the years she never had. Who can tell what happens in the heart and mind of a woman who gives everything but finds no new horizons after children grow and leave. Perhaps there is a loss and a loneliness too great to bear: at least that is how I read it, for Phyl opted out.

Whether it was a pact between two people who needed the heavens to play with I do not know, for this last act in the play was not my theatre — Frank and Phyl left together, she first. When his heartbroken cry came to me that Phyl had died by her own hand, I knew that he was determined to follow her lead, the act of a very brave man who could not live in the world of his choosing.

It is hard to tell the story of a couple who have committed suicide; nevertheless, I am the only one who could be their apologist. Who knows which step leads us where, nor can anyone completely share the heartache of another or allocate blame when we do not know.

McINTOSH

Some fellows like to hear themselves talk — you have heard the proverb "The empty vessel makes the most sound". Mac was not like that, he was the quiet type, stuttered a bit, a private man — lived alone, or so I thought.

His address was Olive Downs, via Tibooburra, probably one of the loneliest addresses in Australia. He had come to town and so had I which is probably why he recognised a camp fire man and stopped to exchange greetings. I was drifting, looking for a job and told him why, which opened him up about his address and a talk about his dogs and his horses, all heavy subjects with a bushman. "Next time you come down you might have a job, and I hope your son gets his eyes fixed. I'll look you up." My son Ian was in hospital with trachoma, that curse of the desert country from which we had come.

When Mac found me a year later there had been several jobs, but none to my liking — for instance, the one carrying bricks in the hod up a ladder, and mixing mortar for brickies who yelled "Hod of mort", putting much sarcasm into the words to let me know how poor a labourer I was. But now I was making packsaddles, part-time, in my back yard.

Leather — that was something all bushmen associated with and we talked leather. Mac had ideas about making boots for dogs to wear in bindi-eye country; about how a legging should fit; about saddles; about cold nights on watch — no trouble now for Mac to talk, he did not even stutter much. Thus foundations of friendships are made — this one lasted.

Something of a philosopher was Mac. He was older than me which meant that I did not ask questions, so it was sixty years later that I learned that Mac had been married. Mac had wondered a lot and, with me as listener, he wondered aloud. Did I believe that a fellow had an unspoken aura, a sort of halo that spoke louder than words, sort of truth thing that allowed no hiding? Were women's ambitions different to men's, and why? A loaded question, this. Mac reckoned a man only wanted to make his way, make good, get along,

I ONCE MET A MAN . . .

prove himself, but a woman only wanted children. Me not having experience this was a one sided argument but it has left a question to be answered.

For anyone bothering to ask the questions, a man alone has lots of thinking and wondering to do. Mac had time to watch nature at work; the survival of the fittest; the cruel ruthless elimination of the weak; the pitiless harshness of the barren land in which he lived, where adjustment to conditions meant life or death. Everybody in the cities seemed to have so much, grow so soft compared to the scorching sun, hard water, wearying distance making contacts impossible for the people back of Bourke — another world. Mac added another dimension to my life, the good ideas about what was needed for a bushman, the questions a lone man asks to an empty sky.

Sixty years after my first meeting with Mac came a ring from Panama, in America. "My name is McIntosh," said the voice. "My father is dead, but I was born at Olive Downs and Dad said that he would like me to meet you some day. My father always talked about how I should meet you if I could — see you in Australia soon."

I know now why Mac pondered his first question about women.

TRELOAR

L ooking back to the time when the Stockman's Hall of Fame was just a dim idea, in the back of my mind was the story an old man told me of his youthful adventures and the years in between then and old age; a saga of great endeavour, great struggle, noble defeat and, at last, a lonely camp far away from towns or cities, perhaps one of the loneliest places on earth. The Hall of Fame was to be a remembrance for him and those who, like him, had lived through struggle and despair to leave their footprints in the sands of time. This is the story.

It was night at Ernabella, then an unknown water at the eastern end of the Musgrave Ranges. We, that is my boss and I, had ventured out past the last of the settled country and, finding water, whooshed down our camels, hobbled them and lit our fire. We had water and wood and packbags full of rations for the months to come, a comfortable feeling. We believed that the nearest white man was many long miles away, and that any other camp fire had to be tribesmen, uncontaminated people of the western deserts who, at that time, had not yet contested their ownership with settlers. This was an Aboriginal kingdom.

As the night came on, a faint glow showed through the blackness of the distance and continued to glow steadily, requiring investigation. It was a kerosene lamp in a small white tent, and by its light an old, white-bearded man sat and read. "Catching up," he said, "on a lifetime too busy to read." That was sixty-four years ago, and Treloar was old then, perhaps eighty, making his year of birth about 1840.

About 1860 he had taken a dray pulled by bullocks and loaded with provisions and had set out from Marree in South Australia to find a place in the then unknown interior. Explorers came after. Passing what is now Oodnadatta, he found good grass north of the Alberga River and decided to settle there. His voice was still strong and his keen old eyes alive with remembrance. Treloar told his tale of the years when he took breeding cattle from the south and built up a herd of cattle at what is now called Eringa. The place seemed well enough watered until the great drought in 1902, when all life perished on Eringa. He walked out empty handed, not even a bullock to pull his dray.

Later Treloar went south, married and raised a family. I never asked the reasons he left the south: one only has to pen a wild horse off the range or release a scrubber cow to know where the wild things go — they go back to the wild, and so did Treloar.

Many years went by and the Stockman's Hall of Fame became a possible reality. Letters from the pioneers' families came pouring into the office, telling about their forefathers, and strange to say came a diary written in Treloar's own hand, concerning the bitter years and the story of the selling of Eringa.

I ONCE MET A MAN . . .

If we do nothing else in the Hall of Fame but remember these great hearts we will not have failed.

A lot of men, yes, and some women, are romantic at heart; like to believe that they could live in the blue yonder among the trees, have distance around them, wind in their face and nobody to bother them. Perhaps the need for such comes from generations of cave dwelling, some long ago, almost forgotten habit that a million years of camp fire and roaming bred, that feeling not yet totally lost in a few generations of city living.

Treloar was like that with a difference — he was an old man when I met him, all alone, just chance that somebody disturbed his solitude. Without I had seen the twinkle of his camp fire in the night, I could not have met him nor would his peace have been disturbed, nor his story told.

DANIEL GAYNEY

Cleaning out my old files, two handwritten letters on bold expensive paper attracted my attention, dated about the early fifties, signed Daniel Gayney. I remembered him as a great man, the friend of presidents, holder of large estates — fabulous estates, so elaborate that caliphs and kings might have envied his elegant mansions.

His hobby brought us together, the breeding of fine Arabian horses — the best— which, by reason of his unlimited purse, were what he could afford. Being Australian held some romantic nuances for Daniel who must have remembered times of romance on the R and R of adventurous war years in the Pacific. Gayney's lifestyle reminded me of the biblical quote: "In my father's house are many mansions." His were scattered over the United States, each excelling the other in opulence, which to a poor Australian were breathtaking, more so to be accepted in them as an honoured guest.

Men of Daniel's self-made affluence do not lose their habits easily (the leopard cannot shed his spots, hidden a bit, but still there under the golden cloak). Our business was about a stallion I wanted, the best he had, which meant dickering over what might be available. His interest could have been nostalgia for Australia or spreading the stallion's blood lines, his breeding creation around the globe. Some men having climbed the pinnacle of wealth need next the accolades of success — a great name. Selling his blood lines across the Pacific could have appealed. My genuine protest of poverty needing something less than the highest priced stallions brought the comforting declaration of brotherhood: "Let us not talk money, there is no need of that between us."

After the Japanese butler, the starched pinafore maids, cooks, and careful preparation for an evening of reminiscences, after fine wines, old port, we settled down to hear Daniel's life story. Not often does one have the chance to learn the steps — the giant strides — taken by such men, who not only sit at the seat of power but have arrived at such security of wealth that only sharing the tale is left.

Along the way that night I probed the soul of that exceptional American. It developed slowly after political discussion that, like many conservative right-wing wealthy men, Daniel had a fear of insurrection, that chaos would ultimately ruin the great American dream of stability. Guarding against such a situation was a priority with Daniel Gayney. About midnight, when our mutual conviviality had reached the stage of Dan and Reg, Gayney went to a hidden safe, a strongroom that would have suited the Bank of England, produced a linen bag of jewels, cut and uncut gems of extraordinary perfection. "These," said Daniel, "are my insurance. Come what may, I can carry my fortune with me."

Daniel Gayney is dead these many years but those two letters, carefully worded, just said: "I notice that after this long time your account is unpaid. I trust you can manage to correct this."

HARRY ZIGENBINE

Why he came to town I do not know, for Harry was a bush-bred man, out of place in a city — seldom bothered to visit a town, even a Ghan town like Marree. Such visits were well spaced because feed was always scarce on town reserves where a drover's horses would starve.

Harry was a droving man, his wife and family were not kitted to visit towns, but there was a pub in the darker end of Adelaide that catered for such as Harry, a place to drink out a cheque, where elbows on the table was the custom. Word came to me that Harry Zigenbine would want to catch the Ghan train to Marree next day and could I see that he went? His family were parked on the edge of the town at Marree waiting for him — places like Marree don't support game, which is all Harry's family could expect to eat. Getting him from the pub to the train was a major problem, for in his present condition Harry was unwilling and Harry was heavy. That was the first time our paths crossed.

Next was his turn to do me a favour. I had fifteen hundred bullocks on the road from Bedford in the Kimberleys with

Elmer Lewis in charge, contracted to deliver over the border into Queensland, a trip right across the Northern Territory to at least as far as the Georgina River, with possible delivery at Dajarra if there were no buyers. A telegram arrived from Wave Hill station, two thousand miles from where I was in Adelaide: "Can't go any further, come take delivery."

There was no cattle transport in those days, cattle walked. I would need horses, packs, men, cooking gear, a whole droving plant. What to do? Remembering that my old drover friend Harry Zigenbine was living/spelling/waiting at Hidden Valley, only a day's ride from number twelve bore on the Murrunji droving route, I sent off a radio message through the Flying Doctor Service to ask Harry to meet me at number twelve bore on the Murrunji — I would bring packs, bridles, saddles, all plant but the horses. Came a radio message: "Will meet you at number twelve with buggy and twelve horses. Son Andy, daughter Edna can come." We met on the due date, sent the station ute back to Tennant Creek and proceeded through the then untended bottom end of Victoria Downs, where scrub bulls, unbranded cattle, and brumby horses had the run of the country.

This was the last big trip that Harry Zigenbine did; probably the worst for he had cattle burned in the dip at the Rankin where the old arsenic tick dip was too strong. He wired me: "Come at once. Cattle burned in the dip. Expect to lose the lot." I wired him: "Wash them in the waterhole. Can't come sending a nurse." It was best we didn't meet for a while for Harry was angry, but he did drive the cattle through the waterhole with few losses.

Next time we were sitting together in deep, canvas lounge chairs looking at an outdoor movie at Tennant Creek. Came half time we went to the rough hessian enclosed toilet. I noticed

I ONCE MET A MAN . . .

he was in trouble with blood red urine — Harry had lived rough, drank heavy, travelled all the hard roads. This was the end of the road.

Edna took up where Harry left off to become (in my book) the best woman drover in the west — she never knocked a calf in the head, seldom lost a cow, managed the roughest teams on the road. Harry had taught her well.

No Christmas passes without a card from Edna.

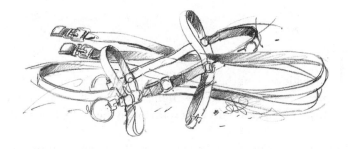

MORTIMER

Lhe shadows lengthen with the ghosts of the multitude we remember marching in the twilight asking to be remembered: just a few, a very few, still wait with me in the land of yesterday.

After fifty-five years, without our paths having crossed since then, my old partner wrote yesterday. In his closing paragraph in a long, well-written hand, he said: "I am in my ninetieth year." The reason he wrote was to bring to my notice that, among other mistakes, the windlass in the Hall of Fame was made incorrectly. How apt, how like the man who stood beside me in the first year of my great adventure, sharing the beginning of an enterprise that became a byword in the outback.

Jim was a man of the outback, manager of Murnpeowie Station in the far north of South Australia — shearing then a hundred thousand sheep, besides carrying cattle and horses — covering millions of wild acres of the desert to Lake Eyre, a vast place, his domain. Jim stood at my humble workbench, nothing more than a board in my father's workshed. Jim knew what I was about: he had heard, as all things on the bush

I ONCE MET A MAN . . .

telegraph are heard, that Dollar Mick, the old half-caste wanderer, had settled to work with a white man camped in the Flinders Ranges, making packsaddles, boots and bridles. This was news to all of the few citizens of the sandhills. Jim came looking, interested enough to want to be a partner in the new venture. We became partners, the price one thousand pounds.

Had he stayed, his sellout price would have been many millions but Jim had other plans — his son wanted a station which is what we arranged. An old territorian bushman had built up a herd of cattle on a piece of Musgrave land which he called Kenmore Park. This he offered, cattle and all, seventy-two windmills, tanks, bores, all thrown in. The house was not much, the cattle numbers unknown, thirty-two thousand pounds the asking price.

Jim bought other places, many places, over the years — took an interest in a multi-storey hotel — his wealth growing with the careful years. Jim still owns Brunchilly Station on the Barkly Tablelands.

Over the half century, we have gone our separate ways but his parting words have stiffened my resolution. "When you need me I will always be there." Jim was — is — that sort of man. Perhaps I have lived my long life in the shadow of his great integrity, not daring ever to betray his trust.

Postscript, June 1989 As I read these proofs, a message has just come through: Jim died today.

I ONCE MET A MAN . . .

AKBAR
AND LALI

I t would not be right to tell the story of Lali without telling the tale of her lifetime lover, Akbar, a young turbanned Mohammedan Afghan, tall, dignified and true to his religion.

Akbar made a few pounds by killing and supplying meat to the outlying mines. His old, borrowed Bedford truck came by regularly to my camp — he sensed a friend, and sometimes stayed to talk. Occasionally after work, or weekends, I would go with him to some far away mine.

This particular night was hot, the highest temperature I have known; 109° Fahrenheit at nine o'clock at night. We had left Yndramindra in the early evening expecting to be at the Lake Carey gold mine before dark but it was not to be; the truck broke down. Our load was two bodies of fresh killed beef, the loss of which would ruin Akbar. He said his prayers facing what could have been Mecca, leaving me to make mine — a wish for a drink, for we had not carried water. In the dark we could do nothing but sit on a log and wait for daylight.

My companion was deeply depressed, not about the spoiling

meat, his concern was for his pregnant wife, Lali — no ring, no papers, no priest, but his woman just the same. As night wore on, Akbar told his story.

Afghan girls were not available (it was 1926) — when camel drivers shipped to Australia from India or Baluchistan, they brought no women. A few married white girls; others mated with coloured girls. Akbar had bought his girl from the tribe — the price had been very high, paid with two camels, some flour and sugar. All had not been well for Lali and him since the purchase — some tribal deal about whose woman Lali should have been, about country they had crossed that a woman should not, probably stirred up by jealous young men of her family.

Being of half European blood but born into a tribal family, Lali had adopted her mother's language and customs out of necessity. She had felt no shame while in the desert about her undressed state — Lali was a child of nature.

Fleeing from what could have been punishment for breaking tribal law had landed Akbar and Lali — now pregnant — into worse trouble when the mission at Mount Margaret took Lali into protective custody. Prudish custom decreed that the female body should be fully covered, so Lali was covered, but the law of 1926 decreed that half-caste women had to be taken into protective custody, which is what the boss missionary did with Lali in spite of Akbar's protests. Lali was sent with police escort to the Moore River settlement in Perth, leaving Akbar lamenting, brooding, and determined to recover his woman. The pain of this injustice was evident as we sat there waiting out the night. Akbar told over and over of his escape from the tribes; it was a long night.

By morning we had gone over the problem to the point of conclusion about what was best to do — self help was

the way to go. Akbar would deliver the spoiling meat, which he did, after we had washed the spoiling taint out with vinegar. He would then proceed to Perth and abduct Lali. We even worked out the calls that would waken Lali from sleep in the night, in the settlement dormitory at Moore River. Lali knew the call of the curlew, her tribal totem. This would awaken her to the presence of her man — the rest was up to her to escape. All this was arranged in detail that hot night by the shore of Lake Carey.

The raid was successful, and Lali was willingly abducted. Together the lovers fled the law, though extradition orders were taken out in South Australia to recover the girl and punish the thief: I have a copy of the extradition papers still in safe keeping. My strategy was to get them a Christian marriage;

and marry them we did; a copy of the 1928 Marriage Certificate is in the hands of their eldest daughter, Mona. Four children were born subsequently to Akbar and Lali at Renmark, South Australia.

Fifty years later Lali went back to the goldfields looking for her long-dead people. Oh, the pathos of that search!

Akbar lies in grave number 62, section M, in the cemetery of Renmark. His religion isolated him from the customs of a people who knew not Islam nor the ways of worship which children of the sun learn in the corroboree, behaviour foreign to a community who bend a pious knee before a man-made altar, or wet a brow in a font of holy water.

Lali lies in an unmarked grave, a child of the wilderness who came like a breath of wind from the desert and, like a wraith visiting another world, briefly returned to her people and her place.

The abduction of Lali by Akbar was never left to rest, and the injustice that parted them and harried these two brave people will forever remain a blot on the treatment of half-caste people in the early years.

THE STORY TELLER

Some families run to champions, at least the Skuthorpes did. Two of the generations I knew were giants in their profession, the taming of horses, which others had given up. Old Lance toured Australia for most of his grown life with a tent show — he was close to eighty when he died, still a straight-backed, tall-in-the-saddle man. Young Lance was cast in the same mould and, like his father, a bare-knuckle fighter, something he practised on the grass outside the circus tent. We were kin with a common interest in the Rough Riders' Guild which made it natural for him to share a trouble with me. The first episode in a chapter of troubles was memorable because it brought us together.

Lance had a habit of driving a taxi for a mate when he was in town, obviously for a quick cash return. The customers sometimes tried tricks to dodge fares, even declaring violence which most cabbies dodge: not Lance — he loved a scrap. This time the fare-dodger had a stranglehold on the driver's neck, and with the cab on a slope and no foot on the brake, the cab was rolling back downhill. The battle continued with

Lance losing the struggle until the inevitable happened — the cab went through a shopfront. Lance was first out and because of a previous charge against him for violent behaviour while in a public facility he chose to vanish.

This was the time we spent most together, for who would look for him in my establishment. We ran and we rode and romped and became fast friends. It was a shame he had to go young, buried now in a foreign land, boots, saddle and whip at his head. Here is a story he left me.

THE ROAD
OF FORGOTTEN MEN

I n the days of long ago, long before the terrifying automobile, before even horse-drawn vehicles could boast of steel springs, men took up selections in the heart of Australia and struggled against primitive conditions to breed cattle and raise their families. Australia was only half taken up then, and although these brave forerunners went right out to the edge of no-man's-land, there was always a forbidding, and inviting Farther Out; forbidding to the weary weather-beaten old man, inviting to the romantic, roving, ever treasure-seeking youth. Many young men, who could not resist the call of the little known Never-Never, rode away from their station homes, and were not heard of again. Some became cattle kings, some master drovers, while others died of thirst, were killed by the blacks, or in the awful loneliness eventually went mad.

There was seldom a night that I didn't sit by the wings of the old stockyard and gaze longingly in the direction of where, since I was a little boy, I had seen many men ride away to a new life, wealth and adventure. There was nothing I couldn't do on a station now, I was eighteen years of age, and had worked with my father and brothers with cattle for as long back as I could remember. There wasn't a horse I couldn't ride or a steer I couldn't throw. I was big and strong, and had come to that time when I felt I must venture forth and fare for myself. I wanted to go out into the back country and take up land of my own to be a great cattleman.

I will never forget the night I broke the news that I was leaving the old home the following day to try for myself. Poor old mother started to cry, my sisters threw frightened looks at each other, and my brother Amos said, "I suppose I'll have to break in the colts by myself. Why don't you wait and see me through with the job?" All eyes were turned towards father as he said, "Well, I can't stop you if you want to go; if I do, you'll only sneak away, anyway. But you want to try and get word back home to your mother and me now and then, and let us know where you are and what you are doing."

Mother said, "Look at poor Dick Marsh and Bob Skinner, and all those other lovely young fellows, just vanished from life. There's terrible hardship out there, men just don't seem to be able to exist in that awful country." Mother went on talking about men who had never been heard of for years as though over the horizon there was a deep dark abyss into which these luckless adventurers unknowingly rode their horses to disappear from life forever. When Mother stopped talking, everyone sat around and gazed into the big open fire in silence for a long time. At length, when the rest of the family had gone to bed one by one, mother and I sat alone.

Mother said, "I wish you were going in the other way, I'll never sleep thinking of you in that wild country. Can't you leave it for another year? You're so young." I only said, "Don't worry about me, Mum, I'll be all right." She didn't say any more, but started to pack my saddlebags with food and little things like a needle and cotton, white rag for bandage, things that only a mother would think of. I watched her as she moved to and fro in the big bush kitchen. What a great woman she was. She came into my room after I had gone to bed and kissed me goodnight without a word.

I was thinking of her next morning as I rode away before sunrise. As I rode through my father's land, the long grass brushed against my stirrups and boots. What a great season it was — cattle crossed in front of me, so fat they could hardly move. Emus and kangaroos were everywhere; wild ducks and scrub turkeys flew overhead and a hundred jackasses laughed together as koalas hurriedly climbed tree trunks and frightened the young galahs.

My packhorse was pulling back on the lead; he didn't want to leave the old home. He, too, was born there. I had to tie his mother to a tree before I left, to prevent her following. I camped that night on a little creek that ran close to the boundary of our land. I knew this creek well, it was an old friend of mine, and this night after dining on smoked beef, johnnycakes and pumpkin pie, I slept like a top all night.

After a week's travel the country had not changed, the same long grass, the same birds and animals and forests of spotted gum, but there was a distinct change of atmosphere — great vastness which made one feel insignificant. I swam rivers and creeks every day, sometimes the same river two or three times as it wound back across my path. I watched the sun from time to time for guidance, and when it was hidden by cloud, I lined up trees in front of me for miles and miles.

For weeks I rode through this tall-timbered, rich country; now kangaroos, instead of dashing through the bush in panic at my approach, would watch me curiously from a few feet as I led my packhorse by and journeyed on into the dim distance.

Most of my food was gone by this, the gun was the tucker bag now. When I was lucky enough to get a turkey I feasted well, but sometimes I had to catch possum. These I roasted over the coals in their skins, Aboriginal style. I had plenty of tea and sugar, mixed together, and flour for johnnycakes and dampers, but these weren't like the roly-polies that mother made so well.

It must have been eight or ten weeks before I started to notice the creeks not half so full, the grass not half so high, and all life except the birds appeared to have vanished.

One day, without warning, I left the bush and rode into open country. It was like a new world; for miles and miles a big plain stretched without even the sight of a stump. Great phantom lakes came right up to my horse's front feet so that with every step I expected a splash of water, but instead, small clouds of fine dust rose to my nostrils and made me sneeze.

There was an indescribable silence out here; it made me sleepy. I don't know how many hours I had been riding across this plain when I discovered with a start that my horse was following a little road. I stopped quickly and looked back. It was like being a long way out at sea, water from the phantom lake appeared to be under my packhorse's legs, as far as the eye could see there was imaginary water. One could almost picture sails and high waves in this strange phenomenon.

In the late afternoon, the phantom lake disappeared to give way to an equally magnificent panorama. Now there was bare ground stretching out to the horizon in every direction, without any obstruction.

I followed the road and camped at a waterless spot long after the sun went down. As I rode on into the next day, the country changed quickly from time to time, until eventually

I ONCE MET A MAN . . .

I left this plain of apparitions and entered the timber again, still following the road. Soon I came to a place where, to my amazement, I beheld a lonely grave under a pretty little tree. I stopped for a while and gazed at it. A small cross marked the spot, and on the tree something had undoubtedly been written but time had healed the wound carved deep in the tree trunk and covered it with bark. This, however, I was tempted to remove, but feeling I was interfering with something sacred, I hesitated and left it hidden in peace. By late afternoon, I had counted six graves all by the wayside, each under the same sort of little trees at various distances along the road. Day after day I rode on, now, in sticky stupefying heat; more little graves by the roadside, still the pretty little trees. The first man I had seen since I left home, gave me quite a shock. I saw him in the scrub about a hundred yards away, staring at me. Suddenly he ran towards me with great speed, stopped when he was within a few feet of me then, to my astonishment, beckoned me and ran backwards into the scrub until he disappeared in the timber.

I was reluctant to follow him, nor was I unnerved by this strange happening — out here one almost expected it. There was an atmosphere of eeriness, I could feel it heavy on me. Never once that day as I rode that road of graves did I feel completely alone. I felt that I was being watched by hundreds of pairs of eyes, curiously peeping at me. The feeling made me almost self-conscious. I straightened my shoulders and shifted my feet backwards in the stirrups until the toes rested correctly in the irons.

Suddenly I came to a man sitting on a log by the side of the road, who had in his hand a bush fishing rod to which was dangling a line, cork, hook and bait. He had just cast the line as I rode up. The bait, which was a big grasshopper,

I ONCE MET A MAN . . .

now rested in the middle of the road. So intently was he watching the cork that he didn't appear to hear or see me. I had stopped and as my horses picked at the edge of the wayside I watched this dry land fisherman, fascinated. As he watched the cork with unblinking eyes, I spoke to him, but he didn't answer. I was about to ride on when I noticed his empty waterbag, so I dismounted, walked to my packhorse, secured a mug, filled it from my waterbag and took it over to him. He drank it dry in great gulps, but never once did he speak or take his eyes from the cork. I was thinking of him as I rode on. What was the matter with him? How did he get that way? Who was he? Was he one of the men I had often heard father and mother talk about? What was the answer to all those little graves along the road?

My thoughts were interrupted as I almost rode abreast of a man riding in the same direction as myself. If he had heard the sound of my horses' hoofs, he wasn't interested enough to turn his head. I slowed up a little and watched him — by this time I was prepared for anything. The horseman rode from side to side as though driving cattle. In his right hand he carried a stockwhip, which he played out lazily from time to time as he left the road as though heading a straying bullock back. His horse was the most magnificent animal I had ever seen, his gear something a young stockman would dream about. He sat on his noble beast like a king and I watched him sway lazily in the saddle. If this man could see stock in front of him, he had better eyes than me, I thought, and so passed him and rode on deep in thought.

The sun was low in the west when I met the next man. He, unlike the others, looked up and nodded when he heard the sound of my horses, as though he was expecting me. He, too, sat by the road, but was very busy carving posts and rails from a deal board of a gin case. Some of these miniature posts and rails were already in the ground, placed beautifully. Each rail was cunningly morticed into the posts. I studied the little stockyard for a long time before I spoke and then, determined to make this fellow talk to me, I dismounted and after removing the bit from my horse's mouth, let him and the packhorse pick by the side of the road.

"Making a model stockyard?" I inquired.

"No, I'm making a tombstone for myself," was the startling answer.

I sat down beside him and watched the tombstone taking shape. How skilful he was, I thought. I was wondering why he was engaged in such a gruesome task when, as though he read my thoughts, he looked up and asked, "Did you see some little graves as you came along?"

"Yes, why?" I said.

"Well there are some smart men buried there, men who came out here years ago. They all went the same way. I'll be with them soon, that's why I'm making this tombstone."

Pointing out towards some old bits of deal board, he said, "Do you see those old boards over there, they have gone black with age; they are off rum and gin cases. This is where we all used to meet the Cobb & Co. coach. Men from stations near and far would ride in to the road and get the mail and drink the grog that Cobb & Co. always brought out twice a year. Some of us came in as far as two hundred miles. We used to meet here and build a big fire. We would hobble our horses out on the creek there, and what a party we would have. Nearly a hundred horsemen, all of us drinking, singing songs, shaking hands and toasting each other. This bad climate made us drink. As time rolled on, none of us ever worried about our mail; we would leave it in the fork of a tree without

I ONCE MET A MAN . . .

even reading it. That's the way you get out here." He pointed to the trees and continued, "Under those trees is where we used to sleep, after the great meeting, then in the morning, we would say goodbye to each other and all ride away in different directions. There are only a few of us above the ground today. Did you see a man riding along the road as though he was driving cattle?"

I nodded. "Well, he was one of the biggest drovers in this part of the country. Like me, he will soon be riding with the phantom horsemen. You'll see them tonight if you're here, the phantom forms of a hundred, and you'll hear them sing bright songs and sad songs like the song of the phantom horsemen, 'We Are Forgotten'."

I sat for a long time thinking of what he had told me, and at length said, "If I was to give you half my pack, and you went back inside, wouldn't you get right?"

"Back in where?" he asked, startled.

"Back in to the Big River, Marree way."

At the sound of those names he cried bitterly. "No, sonny, I've been here too long; I'm doomed," he said at length.

I left him and made my camp about fifty yards further along the road. It was well after dark by the time I made my johnnycakes and ate, and was just making my bed when a great fire that seemed to light up the whole sky make me cower and I watched in astonishment. Smart looking stockmen wearing white moleskin trousers, cabbage-tree hats and blue shirts came out of the scrub on foot in the great illumination. There must have been a hundred of them. They were shaking hands and greeting each other, all obviously in high spirits. In no time a big Cobb & Co. coach drove up. As it came into the light of the fire, the driver coo-eed to the stockmen and they all coo-eed back together. The noise was deafening.

When the coach came to a halt, the stockmen crowded around and lifted the driver from his seat. They and the driver unloaded cases of grog and parcels and bags of mail, then they toasted the driver and sent him on his way. As the sound of the coach died away the phantom forms of the stockmen sang and coo-eed and cheered.

The great meeting kept on for hours, then as the merriment died down, they sang their mourning song, "We Are Forgotten". It was the most beautiful song I have ever heard and easily the saddest. One by one the ghosts vanished and the great fire eventually died down and disappeared with them. In the morning, the still form of the man who had built his own tombstone lay by the roadside and in a little while half a dozen blacks carrying old picks and shovels came out of the scrub and buried him where the little stockyard marked his resting place. And so passed another tired soul, to join the legion of forgotten horsemen.

By now I was a little impatient, and longed for a talk with some normal person. I found one almost that way a few miles further along, in the shape of a publican. As I rounded a bend in the road, I beheld an old public house. It was just a little shingled-roof affair, with a few signs outside about Cobb & Co. and different brands of grog. There was a verandah, and on this sat a man, asleep in a greenhide armchair. I tried to stir him two or three times before I entered the bar, but he snored on in deep slumber and was disturbed not at all by my efforts to awaken him, or by the flies that played leap-frog in large numbers around his closed eyes and open mouth. At the sound of a soft step, I looked up into the frightened eyes of a beautiful half-caste girl who, I was sure, was about to tell me something when the publican appeared on the scene and she, with the grace of a black snake, slid noiselessly through the door without a word.

I ONCE MET A MAN . . .

The publican said, "Good day," and went straight past me to where both my horses were tied, and started to feel their legs carefully as though looking for splints.

"They aren't for sale," I told him. Without looking up from his examination, he replied, "They all say that."

I was a little bewildered and walked into the bar. He was there almost as soon as me and from the other side of the counter he asked, "Wattelit be?"

"Rum, please," I said.

"What kind?"

"Oh, I don't know, any kind. How many kinds are there?"

"Well, I've got several different kinds. For instance, lighting rum, singing rum, sleeping rum, and buckjump-riding rum . . ."

"How does it affect you?" I asked.

"Well, it just depends on which one you have . . . Now this lighting rum affects a cove funny, like. There was a bloke came in here the other day and had some of it, had about four nips, I think. He just sat down in the parlour there for a long time, very quiet, then, all of a sudden he spotted a blowfly on the window. Well, you should have seen 'im shape up to that fly; he must have fought it eight solid rounds then out through the front door he went, swinging at everything in his path. He disappeared in the bush and we haven't seen him since. Then there's the singing rum — talk about songs, never knew there were so many. This bloke, after he had about three nips, sang and sang and sang until he put his head inside an old tin and went on singing until he sang himself to death. Then there's the mighty sleeping rum. That cove out on the verandah had some about ten days ago and he's been asleep ever since and I don't think he will ever wake up."

"Well," I said, "it must be powerful stuff. What about the buckjump-riding rum?"

I ONCE MET A MAN . . .

"Can you ride a buckjumper?" he said quickly.

"A bit."

"Well, that's the drink for you." With that, he turned around and faced some wicked-looking black bottles, selected one, brushed the dust and cobwebs from it, and proceeded to remove the cork which was wired down to the bottle with thick wire. When the wire was loose, he grew very tense and stretched his arms out full length. There was an explosion and the cork went through the roof like a bullet. From the top of the bottle there appeared a blended, blue and purple vapour which climbed swiftly toward the new hole in the roof, made by the cork in its hurried flight. After he had poured me a nip, I grabbed the bottle and slid it over to him significantly, but he shook his head and said, "No thanks, I can't ride." So I sank the nip alone, and asked for another. After I had three of what the publican called "rums", I decided to go into the parlour and rest in one of the comfortable looking greenhide chairs, but he held up his hand and said, "Have one on me before you go." I had the "one on him" as he put it, and then sat me down in the parlour and rested for about an hour.

I was thinking of my mother when the half-caste girl slid noiselessly into the parlour and said, "You go quick, go from here; this man bad man, you die like all other young bloke — go quick." She vanished again as the publican entered the parlour and asked, "How do you feel now?"

Without waiting for a reply, he bent down confidentially and said, "There's a man out in the bar with a big red beard. He owns a horse tied up outside and he'll back it for twenty quid to throw any man in the country. Do you think you can ride him?"

Now very affected by the rum, I said, "Yes, ride any horse in Australia."

Still talking in low tones, he said, "Well, we'll set him, and I'll go you halves with the bet."

"Right," I said and gave him ten pounds.

In due course the money was put up, and I asked the man with the red beard, "Where's your horse?"

"He's tied up outside."

"Well, let's get it over with, and have a drink," I said. The three of us then walked up to the horse. He was a big grey, and I untied him.

"Will you use your own saddle, or the one that's on him?" asked the publican.

"The one that's on him," I said, and looked at the girth and crupper — the latter I let out a couple of holes. I then led the big horse over to a clear patch of ground, adjusted the stirrups, and mounted him. I had no sooner touched the saddle than he rose in the air like a rocket, screwing as he went. He rolled, rocked, and twisted, dropped his shoulder and then his stifle. All the time I rode on the flap, and rolled back again. He was scientific and wasted none of his great stamina. I rode him through his storm — it had been a great battle — but just as I thought I had him beaten, he threw himself backwards, suddenly; I knew he was going right over so I slid back to land on my hands and feet. For a split second I saw the great grey form coming down on me but too late, I lacked the strength to get away. There was a blinding flash then darkness.

Through a purple haze I saw the man with the red beard give the publican something, then the bearded man walked over to my horses, untied them, and led them away. As the two horses followed him away from the house, they both turned their heads and looked over to where I was lying on the ground as though expecting me to protest. There was another period

I ONCE MET A MAN . . .

of darkness, then again the purple haze. This time I saw two black boys stripping big sheets of bark from nearby trees. Under a tree, by the side of the road, was a newly dug grave. Now the black boys were coming over to me, carrying with them the sheets of bark. They all looked very frightened as they lifted me onto one sheet of bark and placed the other one over me. Then very slowly they carried me to the new grave, and lowered me into it. The sun went down and as a great moon emerged over the tree-tops, I heard laughter and coo-eeing, faintly at first, then I could hear many voices in song, now more laughter and coo-eeing which swiftly became louder and plainer. I recognised one of the songs as the one the phantom horsemen sang, "We Are Forgotten".

Closer and closer came the voices, then in the bright moonlight there appeared at least a hundred horsemen wearing cabbage-tree hats, white moleskin trousers, and blue shirts. Now the noise of their laughter and merrymaking was deafening, they were riding right up to my grave. When the foremost of the horsemen reached the edge of my grave, the noise suddenly ceased and one man who was leading a beautiful grey mare cried out, "Come on, old man, you must ride with the phantom horsemen." I rose from my grave and, mounting the hack that he held, rode off into the night with them. As we rode, we sang and coo-eed. We were riding along the road that I had already travelled; sometimes we followed a leader and galloped at a terrific pace. As we passed each little grave along the road, one of the horsemen would vanish, until only a few of us were left, and these after passing more graves were also vanishing quickly, too quickly.

. I was soon alone and suddenly to my amazement I found myself in front of my own grave. Tempted by curiosity, I dismounted, walked over to the edge of my grave and looked in. What I saw horrified me; from the four walls of the grave protruded hideous horned heads and hands with long yellow fingernails. In the bottom of the grave was the most hideous of all the heads, a great yellow horn protruding from the centre of its forehead. It winked and leered at me and as if this was a signal, all the heads and hands started to beckon me. The long fingernails moved like the action of the legs of centipedes. I screamed and ran for my horse. I was just about to mount when a hand grabbed me by the back of the collar and dragged me, screaming and kicking back into my grave. Now the hand started to shake me violently. I twisted my head and bit the hand hard. I wish I hadn't because it gave me the most unmerciful smack across the face which awoke me thoroughly enough to see my sisters, brothers, and mother standing around me bed. They were all asking together, "What's the matter?"

I didn't tell them, but looked at Mum and smiled, saying, "Don't worry, Mother, I have changed my mind about going away. I never want to see 'The Road of Forgotten Men'."

M c L E A N

Archie McLean, tall, thin as a post, a saddle man, soft spoken, keen understanding eyes: he lived in the old traditional station style — cookhouse separated from the living quarters by a walkway, meat house close by; long handled pump at the underground tank near the kitchen; large population of blacks within shouting distance; working dogs tied to shelters, all within fifty yards of the kitchen; saddle-horse yards within shouting distance from the house. Archie was a traditional man. All his habits — his walk, his speech, ways of working stock, pack plants — all marked the man he typified, all that was best in the pioneer cattleman. We, his men, worshipped him like a king, which he was.

It was the habit of head office of the Kidman empire to send young lads to such as Archie at Anna Creek to get experience and maybe become part of the vast Kidman cattle empire. Not many made it.

We were saddling up early for the day's work at the home yards — unusual, for most of the work kept us far out on what was, and still is, the largest single cattle station on earth.

Anna Creek itself is 11,500 square miles, five million acres without the outstations. A lad from the city had arrived by train the previous day and had his new saddle ready at the yards. Victor, head stockman, nodded to the boss. "What do we give the lad to ride?" Archie pointed to a dumpy brumby type.

Victor Dumas hesitated, unusual for Victor, he was a very insular man. "That's had no work, quiet but green."

"They will both learn together, Victor," the boss said. We all heard and we knew that although the boss was a good man, there was nothing soft about him.

When all the Kidman top men gathered in 1932 for Kidman's 75th birthday, Archie led the gallop past the stand. He was number one among top men.

MENZIES

When that Labor man Chifley lost his battle with the banks, there were none of his outstanding calibre left in the Party to follow him. The fight was on for power in Canberra. Chifley put his referendum to the Australian people concerning banking, his banking act of 1945 was defeated. Menzies stumped the country in an effort to get power and in 1949 he came to a small country hall where I lived. All the locals turned out to hear this new voice.

I had a mate who was interested in politics and he persuaded me to hear this new voice. My mate, Frank Pascoe, was a naval man. He had resigned his commission and had joined me in my small manufacturing business, bringing the naval discipline and logic to help what was then a real bushman's catch-as-catch-can, rough-run outfit.

The big night came for us to hear the man Menzies speak. We walked up the hill to the small hall and seated ourselves in the very back row. The hall was full and there in the front row were the loud voiced Labor supporters, mostly wardens from the nearby Yatala jail.

Menzies spoke in a jargon of eloquent profundities that went over my head, but I listened. The Labor presence yelled questions that brought sharp, cutting answers and we all laughed, beginning to appreciate the wit and banter of the big conservative. The night wore on and the front bench, tired of being beaten in repartee, finally shut up. "Any more questions?"

The words were a challenge and being a Chifley fan I stood in the dark back corner and put my question, "Sir, your predecessors kept value in the pound. What will you do about keeping the value in our money and stabilising currency?" My question was loaded with a very personal interest because of having just issued a catalogue offering to keep prices steady and to pay freight.

"I assure you, my boy," said the big man, "I will keep value in the pound." A newspaper man sitting near me pricked up his ears, sensing my concern, and next day the paper carried a banner headline: "Menzies will keep value in the pound."

Three years went by, and in the meantime I became close to bankrupt because inflation is insidious and the likes of me don't notice the price of bread — we are too busy trying to do what we have to do. But the banker was worrying me and the accounts were getting further and further behind. Election time came around and, as if by a coincidence, it so happened that Menzies came to the same small local hall at Northfield (although, I wonder why a man like him would bother). Frank Pascoe and I walked up the hill and took our seats in the same place at the back of the hall. There were the same interjectors and the same ebb and flow of repartee at which Menzies, as usual, got the best of the local boys. Menzies had no equal at the push and shove of verbal brawling: he was good. The shouting died and this time I had come armed with the 1949 paper headline, "Menzies will keep value in the pound." Menzies was seated at the back of the platform resting his big head on his hands.

I stood up and in a loud voice announced, "Mr Menzies, you lied to us." The big old head came up with a start. "Yes, Mr Menzies, you lied," and holding up the headline paper which he could not see, I quoted his promise. Quietly he rose from his chair and ponderously walking to the front of the stage he lifted his head boldly and said, "Yes, my boy, for various reasons of political expediency I did let the pound depreciate." Stopping then for effect, he continued, "But, I did give you more of them." True — again he had beaten the local lads, but I had another question which for the moment was not on my tongue and so we all walked out as the meeting was over. Outside the locals gathered in groups, as men do outside churches and socials — there were no women at this political meeting, perhaps Northfield women were not liberated yet. The big man was standing alone. Frank and I edged up and expecting to be an enemy for my obvious rude remark in the meeting was encouraged by a smile and almost fatherly pat on the head. "Sir, will you tell me now what you will do about the inflation of money?"

Menzies' answer was deliberate and prophetic. "The inflation rate will be kept at a possible level of four per cent! Will that help?"

"Thank you, sir. I am sorry now for my rudeness and can assure you that in future your photo will hang on my wall."

Menzies was a great man — but he was wrong about the four per cent.

YEMARGEE

Interesting that in my own time a man of the horse-and-buggy days could meet a Stone Age primitive; such was the case when I met Yemargee. If that was not absolutely the correct name, it was what I called him.

The people of the Musgrave tribe had met with the scattered Aboriginals from south-west and south to the Nullarbor, west to the Gibson Desert, and north as far away as the Petermann Ranges. Meeting place was a large waterhole called Erli Wanga Wanga, where game was plentiful owing to recent rain — rabbits in abundance, fat kangaroos, emus and wallabies, with grass seed already filling out the harvest. By chance, Bill Wade and I arrived at the waterhole at evening when the big gathering was, in full progress. Women had been digging out rabbits from as far as ten miles along the range and there was roasted kangaroo, enough to feed the multitude. It was a vast gathering, perhaps the last ever of its kind.

We were not welcome; nevertheless, next day the young men took me hunting — bare feet essential, for the slightest sound will alert game; I with no weapon, they with spears.

YEMARGEE 155

By noon the party settled down on a rocky slab where water had gathered in a depression. The boys quickly made fire by rubbing their spear throwers across a crack in a dry log which was filled with very dry kangaroo dung; the hot dust fanned into flame, taking not more than ninety seconds. The rabbit cooked (singed would be a better word) and was eaten as was, almost raw. Because game scares quickly, a large gathering of tribesmen cannot stay many hours in one place. Within three days all were dispersed — our way lay west. Yemargee and his boy, about ten years old, attached themselves to us — it was pleasant company for me for Yem was a great hunter. He would see a wild dog (dingo) far off, planning at sight to approach it close enough to spear; using wind, terrain, cover, he made his approach with stealth until the fatal spear could be hurled — he seldom missed — usually through a vital part.

To use a spear like that became an obsession with me, it was no trouble to learn to get close to game, different entirely to learn to throw a spear which is an art — takes a lifetime. Yemargee seemed not to mind our company or where we went — he could hoist a huge log, too big for me, putting it on his shoulder to carry for firewood, a night log. He talked cheerfully about the tracks of people and animals as we went along, sometimes hard for me to understand but good at sign language with me learning his words quickly. His boundary for tribal travel was Operinina, about four days' travel south of Ayers Rock where he passed us over to a young man who seemed to have license to go north-west to the Petermanns, the way we wanted to go.

A strong, genial, happy soul was Yemargee, he taught me a lot. He could stalk a kangaroo in open country; approach

a wild dingo to spear; distance track a lizard across a rock; dig out a rabbit; observe a possum tree; tell the names of those who left only their tracks. Yemargee could read the smoke signals of his people like others read newpapers, sometimes with amazing detail, which to this day seems like telepathy to me. He kept me informed, taught me his skills to the best of my learning ability. While this man camped with us there was never fear of danger — no need to hunt for water, no possibility of lost camels for he knew where they were without looking. It is hard to understand how a white man could perish in the Petermann area when there were kindly men like Yemargee about. Perhaps it was because I treated Yemargee as a great teacher, my brother, my guide, that he felt responsibility to care.

Strange how the events of the past become legends. Today, sixty-two years after Yemargee had left us at Operinina, the story of events of that time were recalled by phone by a grandson of that tribal people. Now a Christian convert, baptised by Wade and a pastor among his people, he told me how the expedition of Wade and myself was recalled by songs that Wade had taught them when he came back to found the Warburton Range Mission.

I could have wished that it was I who had left such a perpetual memorial in the life of those people, long since changed — perhaps not all for the better — but a Stone Age man bearing witness to a prophet of two thousand years ago is something.

F I R S T
H O U S E
THE BUILDER

When a man builds, he is creating something in his own image — when the building is finished the builder can never be the same again. The building is good; it is bad; it is beautiful; or ugly; and the impression stays in some small way in the character of the builder.

I once met a girl who wanted a house — could she build it herself? Being a long time builder of houses, the idea took on with me that this slip of a girl somehow thought she could build a house. Without telling of the pitfalls that people without experience can suffer, I set out the detail of construction. First the land, then the foundations, the damp course, the walls, the roof beams, the roof, the verandahs — all were considered. Nothing daunts the dreamer! If it does the dreamer had better give up.

The bulldozer man came and levelled the land, and the cost was duly noted. It is easy to let the imagination run wild with the smell of newly turned earth on a freshly made house-site, all smooth, and straight, and ready for a house. Squaring up the lines for the foundations is a mathematical obstacle for any man, let alone a soft-handed city girl, but the pegs were hammered into place and the lines measured and squared, and all was made ready. It took weeks but ambition never faltered. The boards in place, the concrete poured and the floor level, filled with fine gravel, it looked great — almost a house. But is that what hope can see? The figures in the book looked like the bank might break but time, given time, there would be money for bricks. Came the bricks, all stacked ready and they stayed like that for a year or more while resolution recovered.

Not a step was made, not a brick was put into place without long and earnest consideration. The girl builder attended school and learned to plaster, studied charts and mastered the art of making cupboards, and criticised her teachers. The hired carpenter took pity on innocence and pitched the roof cheaply; he did what no other builder might do, charged just his time.

Another year and another year went by, the doors and windows all locked on an empty house. I advised that a table and chairs, and a bed might be necessary before she moved in. And what else? "Some books," I said. "You have a larger task now, to begin the furnishing of your mind against the long years ahead."

REG WILLING

It never was enough to find a hard rock mine. Gold does not come in lumps in hard rock; sometimes a spot will show in quartz but in hematite or mudstone almost no gold shows; solid rocks have to be crushed, ground, treated for the very small particles that make up the pennyweights or ounces to the ton. For this, machinery has to be installed, expensive machinery.

We had a mine of doubtful value but the old fashioned pan, followed by portable stamps, proved that the deposits were there. Engineers were contracted, expensive geologists took all the money we had. The law of the stock exchange allowed that shares not fully paid up could be called on to pay an amount up to the full value of the shares — which is what we did. Mede Almond had been secretary for the old Australian Development Company which was no longer called on the daily exchange. We authorised him to advertise the call which brought in some money, the unlucky ones failed to pay and thus missed out on a fortune.

Came a time when our money ran out and to cap our luck, the engineer, a Melbourne man, told us in solemn tones

I ONCE MET A MAN . . .

that the plant would not be working by 17 October when our contract to start producing ran out.

What to do? The other men on the old board were not young any more — I was the only youngster on the five man directorship. They shook their discouraged heads with evidence of giving up. Being young, with exaggerated ideas of my own ability, it came to me to offer to take over the job of setting up the machinery, to produce enough to declare that a start had been made. The four old men agreed to give me complete control. I often wonder if Mede Almond recorded that minute, for that is exactly how the stage was set for a young and brilliant friend of mine to create the miracle needed to start the mill rolling.

The night before the due date when the contract to start producing had to be met, Reg rang me from Tennant Creek. The great bull wheel that turned the crankshaft that swung the stampers to crush the ore had jammed. A powerful pole was needed to rig a strong set of pulleys capable then of releasing the huge wheel which was stuck. I will not put on record how that pole was produced: sufficient to say that Reg was on a plane early next day with a bank manager's signature to say that the plant was working. It was deemed not wise for him to remain on the site.

The mine went on deeper and deeper, getting bigger and richer as it went. The story of how Reg fashioned the pole with which to free the bull wheel is probably in the files of the Mines Department under a heading, "Action against Willing" or perhaps, "Extradition Order". All is long since forgiven.

Reg Willing is an old man now — proud he must be to say "but for me" to those who later made millions from his resourcefulness.

IAN

Most responsible people would like their children to be better than themselves, to be more educated, more prosperous, but most often forget that wisdom is to be preferred, such as is gained by experience and often associated with hardship. With this in mind it was my intention not to fall into the usual pattern of spoiling the children: rather I thought to subject them to conditions that might shape them more effectively than advice.

Eldest son was sent to school barefoot, partly from necessity, partly as the programme of "bringing up the boy". My system of education was turned around sharply when number one son came home demanding boots — no protest of mine helped, son had a reason and explained that I would not understand because "I was married" — a social problem.

Another mistake, more serious this time, was the idea I had of ridding the family of any feeling of inferiority that might have resulted from having been too poor to keep up with the Joneses, the cure being the purchase, on credit, of a noble mansion complete with many bathrooms, sweeping lawns, plus exotic cars. The financial problem was soon cured but the mistake could not be. It soon became evident that a mansion and prosperity create more problems than they cure.

Having a bush background with a wide circle of outback connections, it was my wish that number one son should get bush experience as soon as schooling allowed. This resulted in his being sent up the Darling to an old family of long association with Nappa Merrie Station on Cooper Creek. Next step to Macumba in South Australia, a Kidman place, where Ernie Kemp reigned over a domain of desert land stretching from the Hamilton to Lake Eyre, a vast holding. The Kemps were packsaddle, bronco-ing men, with cattle spread over thousands of square miles in the driest area on the driest continent on earth. The term used is breaking in the boy, no jackeroo homestead-based training for the boys in Kemp's camp: Ern Kemp did not look out over the blue yonder from a verandah — he rode out, a saddle man as Kidman, his master, required.

Came a time when we needed to bring a mob of cattle from Oolloo Station on Pine Creek in the Northern Territory, down to Tennant Creek — a long drive. The road down the telegraph was dry, resulting in a decision by Tom Parker, the droving boss, to take the Dry River track seldom used. The proposed route needed long, explorative trips on horseback to spy out the waters and the grass. Son Ian went with Tom on this lonely, hardly known way, months of true pioneering, with the life of a herd of cattle at stake — Tom Parker, drover, was the best of the breed and any boy who served with him could be proud to have studied under the great master, for the university of the road has degrees that know few professors. I met the mob at Top Springs, then a Murrunji destination on the route from Halls Creek to Newcastle Waters.

IAN

The news must have been a shock to an unwashed droving boy, news that he was to proceed from Newcastle Waters to Alice Springs to Adelaide to Sydney to America. A friend had agreed to place Ian in a prestigious American institution as a scholar and had pull enough to install Ian in Andover, a school noted as being the ultimate in schooling for the sons of the "elite". Hardly a place for a boy with droving clothes, no money, and still with the bull dust of the road; it was tough on the boy but I did not know any better. His American sponsor helped.

Those years were a time of financial restriction in Australia, it was almost impossible to export money. In desperation I carried small bars of gold to sell on the black market in New York, which ripped me off but the case was desperate.

Andover gave way to Massachusetts Institute of Technology in due course; again a scholastic hurdle plus a serious economic squeeze for him and for me. Working early morning in the food hall at MIT helped, besides as Ian confided in me, with the price of steak out of his reach, the food hall provided him with access to the best. Fraternity houses bid for popular boys to share the initiation exam, a sort of gauntlet of impossible tasks like hoisting the MIT flag on top of another university pole or making a speech in favour of prohibition in the streets of the lately free Boston. I can't remember the exact task given but the type of final examination for entrance was the making of a speech on chastity in a brothel: whatever the hurdles, Ian made it.

Graduating as an engineer with a job ahead in the Persian Gulf, my fear was that he might go international with his high degree, which for a time he did, but before he left Australia we saddled up five horses with packs to ride the outback roads looking for a family property. Sleeping out in rain and shine,

I ONCE MET A MAN . . .

number one son saw the best of Queensland, where he left me to settle.

Fever took Ian in Nigeria, two types — both deadly fevers from which few recover: he did.

By this time at home there were wild cattle to catch, timber to clear, fences to ride, houses to build; all heavy handed work that goes to the making of a man. That was thirty years ago and we could well suppose that the task of the making of a man is well on the way: perhaps it could be that the roles are now reversed, or so it seems.

If he fails, do not blame your child for what he is; look first in the mirror and ask, "What was lacking in me?" If he succeeds, be thankful that your prayers did not go unanswered.

THYRZA

Ｐeople with a living to earn keep close to realities — at least most do, and for forty odd years I did. When employing artists from time to time, our requirement was essentially for those who could illustrate in a way that readers could identify clearly and, if possible, admire.

She was young and petite, meticulous in art as in everything else. Her application for a job as an illustrator was a classic copperplate letter, no doubt to emphasise her ability. It stated that she was studying under Ivor Hele who without question was pre-eminent as a portrait painter, and being an admirer of Hele's work I was interested to see what his student would be like. Having a long standing scepticism of illustrative art, I wondered about the hand which had produced the illustrious letter, the kind of writing my father could produce (although he seldom did). "For the writing oft proclaims the man."

It was our custom to print poetry in the magazine *Hoofs and Horns*, sometimes with illustrations. This particular month the poem was Ogilvie's "Jundah's Riding Camel" and the

I ONCE MET A MAN . . .

illustration for it seemed a suitable test for our applicant. The result was better than satisfactory, as our older readers will remember.

Work never seemed to staunch the flow of Thyrza Davey's ambition: her spare time, when most people would have been relaxing, produced copies of the masters — etchings, landscapes, porcelain paintings, there seemed no end to art. She showed promise, although as an admirer of Norman Lindsay some of his more bizarre example showed through. The tedium of magazine illustration bored her but with unending patience she was "toiling upward" — dedicated, inspired, exceptional.

In 1953 with packhorses and no destination, my son Ian and I left Adelaide to look over the cattle lands of northern Australia. Thyrza left Australia by ship for Africa with a view to expanding her horizons. There with saddle-horse, gun and paints she set out to explore the Kalahari Desert. Had her adventure been a hundred years earlier, the pygmy bushmen of the desert might have cared for her. The Kalahari is lonely

now as Thyrza discovered. Not that she cared, for, as with those of her kind, the wind and the far horizons, the whispering voices of empty places, were something of what she wanted.

Rumours reached the police who no doubt relished the idea of searching for a young and beautiful girl, alone in the desert, not caring that she neither wanted to be found nor rescued — nor taken into protective custody, which is what happened. The "being rescued" became a traumatic experience which she could well have done without, for it not only ended a brave adventure but opened doors of bitter experience.

Thyrza's art reflected the change, in strange demonic expressions which I could not then understand — that was a time when criticism was untimely. We make these mistakes.

The years went by, many years. A book of paintings and illustrated story has lately reached me, splendid work in the style of the old masters, signed by Thyrza Davey and a note to RM: "You are long since forgiven."

ROBERT

Ⅰn the new world, and it is a new world, evolved in my short lifetime — when I was a child, the horse and buggy reigned. First the motor car, then the wireless, and now the moon. The change has brought with it many accolades of distinction. The recognitions are not all new — money, titles, art, music, letters — but the emphasis has changed.

In a pioneering society where muscle marked the man there were other standards, other universities where cap and gown give way to earthy values. Robert Sadler graduated in the school where a man "steadied the lead", could ring a mob of wild steers and saddle his own outlaws. I am sure he would spurn a doctorate in philosophy.

Bob was drifting his droving plant horses along the road in 1982 — just letting them grass. Contract droving was almost out just then, the outlook was grim and he showed it — pulled up by my camp looking for someone to complain to. We got around to talking about the weather, sympathising about how hard times were until we ran out of complaints and came to the obvious question: Where would he be going? The

I ONCE MET A MAN . . .

conclusion was that Bob would put his horses in the Hall of Fame's one hundred acres at once in exchange for having him mix mortar and cut stone for me.

Now it takes a big man to hang up his spurs, stack his packs and get down into the bulldust on foot and mix mortar. Could be that having found, at last, someone to agree that droving was a hard life and most bosses were no good, plus a fellow feeling for the camp fire, Bob had a homecoming feeling.

Early mornings, long before first light, I would get a kick in the swag and would wake to find a fire going, the billy boiled, mortar ready — the home feeling was mutual. At smoke-o every day a pot of tea arrived with Betty and her child Danny: very shy Danny, clinging to his mother who was almost as shy. Betty had grown up as Bob's offsider on the road, his eldest daughter. The life on the road with cattle breeds another kind — for girls born to the camp fire there are no toilets, no bathrooms, except the muddy waterholes where privacy is where it can be found in the scrub or behind the tanks at the bore. If a drover's child seems to have different values you are right, they have. This is a different kind of school: not much time for wash days on the road with cattle, or for schooling. These things I knew, for the road and the swag were mine also.

Came a time when the rocks were all laid and the great hand-cut beams that Bob had helped fix in place were roofed. When the marble floor was all laid in cement, Betty would pull Danny around on a mat. It has been said that Betty and Bob were uncouth; I explained it to Bob once that he put his elbows on the table when he ate. So do I — lots of my mates are uncouth, but as we had no table in the camp at that time it was of no consequence.

DANGEROUS
DAN

Some of his experiences had written their stories on his face — Dangerous Dan. Seldom has a man been better named but he did not select the title, he earned it.

Something of his early years are hearsay in western camps, but my meeting took place in the camp of Ironbark Davey. Ironbark, named after the craggy bark of the most durable eucalyptus, a title he deserved, was a man from the sandhill country east of Farina, rugged as they come. At the time he owned Granite Downs, scene of my early years when Mick O'Donohue owned it. Ironbark had reached a time for retirement and his idea of such was to own a small pub on a road where men of his knowing went by. The place was a drovers' camping place, now a motel, eighty miles north of Alice Springs.

For want of something to attract his kin and kind from far places, Ironbark decided to hold a Bush Rough Riding Picnic and he asked me to run it. My advice was to select all the best outlaw horses in the country, bring in a herd of several hundred bullocks and, most important, buy a trainload of hay to feed the animals. I also suggested he build a shatter-proof bar to hold all the heavy drinkers from as far away as the Kimberleys, plus a dance hall to keep the drinkers busy at night, and added that a team of sweepers to look after the broken bottles would be useful. He did all this and more — he built a strong, netted arena, a grandstand, a loudspeaker system, a set of chutes, and, most important, two cold rooms to accommodate several truckloads of beer.

Dangerous Dan was managing The Stirling, a large rangy cattle station, seventy miles north. Dan was to supervise the keeping of the peace — what a choice.

I arrived two days before the big opening, was introduced to the peacemaker by Ironbark and left to get acquainted. First question as Dan looked me over from the back of the horse, comfortable and not bothering to dismount: "What do you know?" A leading question. My answer was another question: "Where are your working horses, pick-up team, dogging horses, roping horses?"

This was not Dan's department, but being what he looked to be and there being no one else to ask, I reckoned that he might have the answers. Dan pointed to a bunch of yarded horses and I looked them over. I had a saddle and proceeded without any more talk to catch and saddle a likely looking mare. Dan was in his element, challenging and as cynical as a man can be to a stranger. "Only broke yesterday; think you might?" He left it at that.

Horses in western camps are all suspect and no man questions what a strange horse might do, with the result that experience teaches that the reins are gathered together with either a handful of mane or by preference the near-side ear and the leg goes smoothly over to meet whatever might happen. I had lately come from my own camp where "forking" colts was the custom and managed to get safely onto the recently broken mare. Dan's critical approval was evident; we had step one to acceptance.

Dan had always tailed his beast rather than pulled it down by the horns, which meant that he had to make his first leap dogging his beast. He liked it and got into the business of picking off riders without seeming to have learned.

The first day of the rodeo wore on and Dan had worn out several horses doing all the picking up or off of the riders who rode their bucking stock. He liked it as, for his efforts, he was rewarded with all the beer he could drink. Towards evening, the mare he rode was blood-stained with spur marks down the flanks — she had only been broken and not worked with the result that she learned the hard way.

A prevention of cruelty type standing at the fence passed rude remarks about the bloodied spurs and Dan took no notice, or seemed not to, until late in the day he cantered his horse at the fence and leaping head first hit the critic as he went. The critic had friends and the situation was not good. It looked all too unequal, a potential massacre, for there could have been men there who had suffered at Dangerous Dan's hands. Among the management there were a few who knew about such things and in a very short time, apart from a few skinned faces and hurt feelings, the riot was over — the peacemaker had justified his position and had added another strong bond with his new friends.

Before Ironbark's big gathering was over and tempers had worn thin, Dan had again lived up to his name as Dangerous and had almost stomped a man to death — we knew his reasons were good but charges of murder are too serious to be hung on mates. We took part.

Much has happened and changed as always happens — nothing remains as it was. Dan and family left the station giving them a chance to attend school. Dan's fighting days are nearly done, but a reputation like his will keep the others careful. At one of our last meetings, Dan told me with deep pride that his eldest son could beat him now and had whipped him.

That's standards for you, the measure of the man.

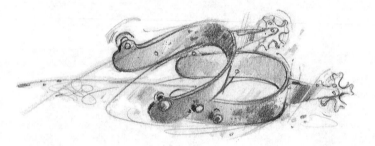

HELL WEST AND CROOKED

TOM COLE

'The Horses are hell west and crooked –
it'll take a week to muster them'

In this remarkable autobiographical account, Tom Cole tells the stories of his life in the outback during the 1920s and 1930s. With great humour and drama, he recounts his adventures as a drover and stationhand in the toughest country in Australia and later on as a buffalo shooter and crocodile hunter in the Northern Territory before the war.

Tom Cole was awarded the Medal of the Order of Australia in 1994 for his contribution to history. First published in 1988, *Hell West and Crooked* has now sold over 100,000 copies.

'A real-life story of the pioneering days of the Top End that out-adventures anything fiction writers could hope to produce.'

The West Australian

'Tom Cole is a living legend, a real-life Crocodile Dundee. His stories paint a vivid picture of wild and exciting times in the Australian Outback.'

Melbourne Sunday Express

'A story of the outback and cattlemen and women, stripped of glamour, that will become an Australian classic to rub covers with authors like Ion Idriess.'

Gold Coast Bulletin

THE LAST PARADISE

Tom Cole

'Crocodile Dundee has nothing on Tom Cole.'

Sunday Sun

Tom Cole hunted crocodiles and buffalo, was a horse-breaker, brumby runner and drover, owned and managed cattle stations and a coffee plantation.

The Last Paradise is the sequel to Tom Cole's bestselling autobiography *Hell West and Crooked* and recounts his story of thirty years in New Guinea amongst 'crocodiles, cannibals and coffee'.

Operating as the first professional crocodile shooter in New Guinea, Tom Cole risked life and limb hunting from frail canoes in wild and sometimes unexplored country, working with everyone from cannibals to missionaries to government officials, and the larger-than-life characters still drifting around the Pacific after the war.

Tom Cole, Australian legend, led a life like no other.

Sequel to the bestseller *Hell West and Crooked*

RIVER OF GOLD

HECTOR HOLTHOUSE

The Wild Days of the Palmer River Gold Rush

'What with cannibal blacks, pig-tailed Chinamen in thousands, lynch-law hangings, gambling dens, shanty towns, murders, grog-shops and Italian opera singers, the Palmer River goldfields – properly spun out – should provide enough television material for general exhibition for the next ten years. This one book, *River of Gold*, could easily be used as the jumping-off ground for the lot. Read it with Hector Holthouse; he will be your guide; he has loved every minute of it, and so will you!'

Canberra Times

'The gold rush at Palmers River, on Cape York, lasted about seven years in the 1870s, but with 35,000 diggers it was this country's wildest while it lasted. Holthouse has researched the story of those days well to make a lively and very readable book.'

The Bulletin

S'POSE I DIE

HECTOR HOLTHOUSE

'This English girl will never stick it out,' said one of the bridegroom's friends when Evelyn Evans arrived in Cairns in 1912 to marry Charles Maunsell. She went from a comfortable house near London to an isolated Mount Mulgrave homestead with unlined roof and antbed floors. For months in the wet season the station was cut off from the outside world, and more than once in the lonely weeks when the men were away mustering Evelyn Maunsell came near to death from illness of marauding Aborigines.

Hector Holthouse, author of a number of books on Australian history, was born on Queensland's Darling Downs. He became a sugar chemist and spent several years in the north Queensland sugar belt, during which time he became interested in the colourful history of the north. The first of his Australian histories, *River of Gold*, is an account of the Palmer River gold rush.

S'pose I Die is about the same country, after the rush was over and beef had replaced gold as its main export. It is based on Eve Maunsell's written recollections and on her conversations with Hector Holthouse about her life in the Mitchell River country and on the Atherton Tableland.

'an enthralling story'

The Telegraph

'a lively and readable account of a pioneer woman's life'
The West Australian

GYMPIE GOLD

HECTOR HOLTHOUSE

For fifty years after James Nash discovered gold in 1867 at the spot on the Mary River in Queensland where Gympie now stands, gold was the town's main source of income. And in that period the lure of a fortune was responsible for many dramatic events – the sensational Escort Murder, hold-ups by bushrangers, battles between Chinese and European prospectors – which Hector Holthouse vividly describes against a background of life in a frontier town with all its hardships.

Illustrated with photographs and drawings of the period and the author's own photographs of present-day Gympie, *Gympie Gold* is popular history at its most readable.

Hector Holthouse, author of a number of books on Australian history, was born on Queensland's Darling Downs. After working as a boy on the family farm he became a sugar chemist and spent several years in the north Queensland sugar belt, during which time he became interested in the colourful history of the north. He served in the Australian Army Education Service in World War II and later wrote for the Brisbane Telegraph and was a part-time university lecturer in journalism. His other works include *River of Gold*, an exciting account of the Palmer River gold rush, *S'pose I Die, Up Rode the Squatter* and *Cyclone*.

THE TERRITORY

ERNESTINE HILL

Timeless because it is history, timelessly popular because it is so full of life, colour and adventure, *The Territory* is the story of the first hundred years of white exploration, pioneering, and settlement in Australia's tropic north. Based on the author's first-hand knowledge and experience, this is the result not only of years of research but of thousands of kilometres of strenuous travel.

Cattle-droving over unknown wildernesses, tragic encounters with Aborigines, the efforts to establish settlements that were cut off from the world and inevitably covered by the relentless growth of vegetation, the first crossing of the continent, the building of the Overland Telegraph line, and the incredible lives of men and women of three generations – this is the stuff of *The Territory*.